A Practical Application of Supply Chain Management Principles

Also available from ASQ Quality Press:

The Supplier Management Handbook, Sixth Edition
ASQ Customer–Supplier Division; James L. Bossert, editor

Managing Contract Quality Requirements
C. Robert Pennella

Managing Service Delivery Processes: Linking Strategy to Operations
Jean Harvey

Value-Driven Channel Strategy: Extending the Lean Approach
R. Eric Reidenbach and Reginald W. Goeke

The Executive Guide to Understanding and Implementing Lean Six Sigma:
The Financial Impact
Robert M. Meisel, Steven J. Babb, Steven F. Marsh, and James P. Schlichting

Transactional Six Sigma for Green Belts: Maximizing Service and
Manufacturing Processes
Samuel E. Windsor

Managing the Customer Experience: A Measurement-Based Approach
Morris Wilburn

The Desk Reference of Statistical Quality Methods, Second Edition
Mark L. Crossley

Lean Kaizen: A Simplified Approach to Process Improvements
George Alukal and Anthony Manos

Root Cause Analysis: Simplified Tools and Techniques, Second Edition
Bjørn Andersen and Tom Fagerhaug

The Certified Manager of Quality/Organizational Excellence Handbook,
Third Edition
Russell T. Westcott, editor

Enabling Excellence: The Seven Elements Essential to Achieving
Competitive Advantage
Timothy A. Pine

To request a complimentary catalog of ASQ Quality Press publications,
call 800-248-1946, or visit our Web site at http://www.asq.org/quality-press.

A Practical Application of Supply Chain Management Principles

Thomas I. Schoenfeldt

ASQ Quality Press
Milwaukee, Wisconsin

American Society for Quality, Quality Press, Milwaukee 53203
© 2008 by ASQ
All rights reserved. Published 2008
Printed in the United States of America
14 13 12 11 10 09 08   5 4 3 2 1

Library of Congress Cataloging-in-Publication Data

Schoenfeldt, Thomas I., 1946–
   A practical application of supply chain management principles / Thomas I.
Schoenfeldt.
      p. cm.
   Includes bibliographical references and index.
   ISBN: 978-0-87389-736-5 (alk. paper)
   1. Business logistics. I. Title.

   HD38.5.S35 2008
   658.7—dc22   2008001858

ISBN: 978-0-87389-736-5

Publisher: William A. Tony
Acquisitions Editor: Matt T. Meinholz
Project Editor: Paul O'Mara
Production Administrator: Randall Benson

ASQ Mission: The American Society for Quality advances individual, organizational,
and community excellence worldwide through learning, quality improvement, and
knowledge exchange.

Attention Bookstores, Wholesalers, Schools, and Corporations: ASQ Quality Press
books, videotapes, audiotapes, and software are available at quantity discounts with
bulk purchases for business, educational, or instructional use. For information,
please contact ASQ Quality Press at 800-248-1946, or write to ASQ Quality Press,
P.O. Box 3005, Milwaukee, WI 53201-3005.

To place orders or to request a free copy of the ASQ Quality Press Publications
Catalog, including ASQ membership information, call 800-248-1946. Visit our
Web site at www.asq.org or http://www.asq.org/quality-press.

Printed in the United States of America

 Printed on acid-free paper

Quality Press
600 N. Plankinton Avenue
Milwaukee, Wisconsin 53203
Call toll free 800-248-1946
Fax 414-272-1734
www.asq.org
http://www.asq.org/quality-press
http://standardsgroup.asq.org
E-mail: authors@asq.org

Table of Contents

List of Figures and Tables

Preface

After years of teaching this type of material and reviewing many different books, I was unable to locate one book that covered the topic in the manner that I was thinking. As a result you now have the consummation of my efforts from many years of work.

The principles discussed in this book have been proven to work and create value-added results in many different industries. As these concepts were being screened and developed so that they work effectively, there was a learning curve involved and I had much to learn. As you read and study this book, I trust that some of the content will also be challenging to you, but that you will be able to apply some of these principles in your profession and make the world a better place as a result.

The principles that are described in this book are the ones that I have been using in my consulting business for more than 10 years. This is not an all-encompassing consolidation of all the possible tools and principles. There are other authors that have taken the specific concept approach and have done a very good job. This book is designed to give you a good applicable understanding of the topic of supply chain management.

As you read this book your mind will be challenged to try new ideas and even refine some of the concepts described. Enjoy the book and use the new knowledge that you have obtained.

Acknowledgments

I would like to acknowledge the many people that I have worked with in the preparation of this material. These are colleagues at the organizations where I did consulting, as well as my fellow members in the Customer–Supplier Division of ASQ. These folks helped by encouraging me to continue on with the effort to learn more and expand my knowledge of this subject.

I would like to acknowledge Madonna University for allowing me to develop this material for workshops, and my students for being willing to try to apply these techniques.

I would also like to acknowledge the endurance of my wife, Carol, as she had to live with me through the development of these concepts and in many cases be my sounding board for different ideas. She was a great help and support in this project.

I would also like to acknowledge my friend Dr. Andrea Vincent for her help in the editing process.

I would also like to acknowledge the staff at ASQ Quality Press and New Paradigm for their help in this project.

Thanks to everyone who helped play a part in the development of this work.

Introduction

In years past, customers were able to drive the prices and deliveries of their materials. This was possible in a domestic economy. With globalization increasing more and more each day, customers must begin to build relationships with their suppliers and practice effective supply chain management to maintain the supply of essential materials.

With the signing of the NAFTA agreement in January 1, 1994, the United States saw its industry base change. Many companies created operations in Mexico because it was cheaper and more profitable to operate there. Today we are seeing another business shift. This time it is from Mexico and the United States to China and India. As these shifts occur, the countries' economies are changing as well. Countries that are securing new businesses are getting stronger while those that are losing businesses become weaker.

These changes prompt significant questions: "If a company had been managing the supply chain, would the business be moving?" "If a company works to develop healthy suppliers, will the operations remain nearby?" These are very tough questions that seem to have been ignored by many U.S. companies over the years, when the focus was on price alone.

Can the trend to keep moving operations offshore be reversed? I believe that it can, but it will require a change in the way many U.S. companies are currently doing business. As we look at the subject of making the needed quantum leap by managing the supply chain, we will see an opportunity to develop and maintain efficient and competitive businesses within the United States.

This book is designed to share the principles of *supply chain management*. It is written based on the practical experiences of the author, relating them to industry principles that are discussed in the various chapters. This book can be used as a textbook for business education or as a reference book for businesses that recognize the need to change the way that their supply chain processes are managed.

Chapter 1 evaluates business developments over the years to demonstrate how the trends have gone almost full circle. Many companies have not learned from their experiences. We present examples of how businesses were driven a few years ago compared to how they are driven today.

In Chapter 2 we will define the supply chain and the companies involved, and show several examples. In addition, we will discuss the development and effective use of process mapping. A complete supply chain and process map of a specific organization will be presented in order to introduce the supply chain concept. This will help identify who the players might be for your organization.

Chapter 3 helps develop the supply chain management strategy within an organization. A supply chain maturity model has been created that can be used to determine where different organizations are in the process. In this chapter, forecasting and other areas dealing with the customer are discussed. This will help you begin to think about your organization and what changes might be made. An evaluation will be presented to help a company assess themselves as a customer. Would you want to be your own customer? This evaluation will help visualize what a good customer looks like for your particular company.

Chapter 4 discusses the decision of whether to make or buy. This is the first step in supply chain management.

In Chapter 5 there is a supplier selection process to help identify the best supplier for the organization in its present situation. This detailed method works well regardless of volumes and prices by considering many variables that companies encounter when dealing with members of the supply chain.

Having selected a supplier, Chapter 6 introduces a procedure for their effective implementation. This is the beginning stage of the supplier certification process.

Chapter 7 describes international situations and how to effectively build international relationships. Culture is a very important aspect of international relationships that must be considered in supplier relationships. The issues of globalization and international relationships will be discussed, as well as the impact that different cultures and companies can have on supply chain management.

In Chapter 8, we begin to consider relationship building. Initially, we will look at relationships from many perspectives. It is important to determine who should be involved, how teams should be arranged, and the scope of the work that the teams can do.

In Chapter 9 supplier quality system surveys are discussed, with examples. Supplier visits are addressed, and we will explain both how to run a visit and the results that might be expected from the supplier.

Chapter 10 discusses scorecards and measures of suppliers. The concept of the seven-part *total perfect order* is presented and how this can help both your organization and your supplier to improve.

Chapter 11 focuses on customer satisfaction. This incorporates a discussion of where different quality standards fit into supply chain management. Currently, there is a disconnect in this area in many organizations because quality subsists as a discrete department that is weakly related to other areas of the organization. Customer satisfaction is one area that is called out in the quality standards.

Chapter 12 describes some quality tools and explains how they can be applied to supply chain management. The details of how to develop these tools can be found in other texts; we concentrate on their applications.

Chapter 13 discusses two of the hot topics in supply chin management today: inventory and logistics. These areas can involve significant investment and so they need to be managed as part of the supply chain.

Chapter 14 covers information systems and some applications that can help in supply chain management. This is an overview of software packages that does not promote specific vendors. The primary focus here is how information technology can help manage the supply chain.

In a postscript (Chapter 15), taking the supply chain management to the consumer level is discussed with some personal examples. It is essential to remember that each of us are both customer and supplier. In either circumstance we want to be treated well and so we should return the same behavior.

As you read this book, think about the concepts presented in terms of how they might be implemented in your organization to make it better and improve the supply chain management process. I trust that this will be a learning journey for you as you read and apply what is in this book.

Thomas Schoenfeldt

1

The Way Things Were (Are)

Costs were more important than quality in the late 1970s and early 1980s, and now again in the early 2000s. When senior management focuses on costs, the supplier that can provide the material at the lowest price is always selected. Many times suppliers have had to cut corners to make any profit and still keep the business running. Often these corners are cut in the quality arena.

The focus on costs became more prominent because the managers' incentive programs were based on cost performance. One company that I worked with had a standard cost system that calculated the amount of money that should have been spent based on the production achieved. The standards were based on historical data and calculated by regression analyses with multiple variables. These cost systems took into account all the costs involved in the specific operation or product. Computer programs performed all of the calculations and prepared a detailed report that included any variances between the actual and the predicted costs. Variances had to be explained to senior managers at least quarterly and at larger plants monthly. Many of these standard cost systems were developed using historical data spanning about five years. An arbitrary improvement factor was incorporated into the current cost calculation in an attempt to force the process to become more cost-efficient. These rates—the improvement factor—were adjusted every year with the goal of improving cost performance and plant efficiency without changing the system. Some improvements could be achieved by eliminating waste from the system, but without systemic changes major breakthroughs could not occur. As Dr. Deming and Joseph Juran would have said, management controls the system and management must be the ones to change it.

Dr. W. Edwards Deming was one of the quality gurus in the 1950s and 1960s who used statistics to understand the performance of processes. Deming's process became known as *statistical process control* or SPC. His

1

mission became to spread the gospel of quality management. Dr. Deming's theories were aimed at the top management of an organization.

Joseph M. Juran was another of the quality gurus of the same era as Dr. Deming. Juran developed the *quality trilogy* of *quality planning, quality control,* and *quality improvement* to help organizations reduce costs that can be associated with poor quality.

Going a step further, the cost standards only measured operating performance with no regard for quality or overall yield. A manager could push a lot of material through a process and look good from a cost basis even though the product was substandard and/or required rework. This could easily happen in intermediate process steps where the material is passed on to another process.

The next phase that came about was called *raw material standards,* which were a material balance, also called a mass balance, applied around the entire operation, with standard yields that were based on a five-year history of the operation. Again, these yields were developed by using historical data and applying an improvement factor. Hypothetical values were also calculated for any chemical reactions so an assumed number was the theoretical standard. Process results could be evaluated as to how close they come to the theoretical best possible performance.

The cost (operating costs that are controllable at the plant level) portion of the standards amounted for about 30 percent of the costs while the raw materials amounted to nearly 70 percent of the costs. By using both of these methods, the system of standards dealt with the total costs for running an operation. At this point, the purchase price of the raw materials was used as the standard since purchasing was handled by a centralized purchasing organization. The plant had no control over the price paid for raw materials; the only costs they could control were the operating costs determined by the efficiency of the plant.

The purchasing managers were the individuals who interacted with the suppliers, and they contacted the sales representatives or the order desks. This was the only point of contact between the company and suppliers. Requests for new or replacement materials and parts depended on the purchasing department to locate a supplier and place orders. Purchasing managers drove their operations under a system known as *purchase price variance.*

This system began with the purchasing department compiling an annual budget for raw materials based on estimates provided by manufacturing management. The total cost of these materials was then used as a point of reference for the incentives that were paid to the purchasing managers. If purchasing was able to buy materials cheaper than the estimates they could earn a substantial bonus. The lower the total final costs, the larger the bonus they would receive. Specifications were very loose and so quality was not considered in the purchases—only the costs dictated the purchasing decisions. Thus, if it could be purchased cheap, the plant would have to use it. Most of the purchasing staff had never even visited a plant so they had no idea what factors were important to the plant and its operation. The only individual at the plant who had any role in purchasing was the one who released orders for raw materials as needed to the centralized purchasing office.

To ensure that the plant was getting the best price, the purchasing department used many suppliers and had them bid against each other to drive the prices down. In many cases, unhealthy suppliers arose and no consideration was given as to how these suppliers were treated. Purchasing was instructed that the plant must never run out of material. To protect themselves, purchasing used several suppliers, thus ensuring that material would be more readily available in the case of poor planning.

Businesses were run with a focus on production, driven by the idea that if you could produce more material it would sell. The senior management wanted more, more, and more from the same amount of people and resources. If the workers worked harder, more production could be achieved. No consideration was made for the limitations of the system.

Incentives were paid to the managers based on output, while many of the workers saw no benefit from their efforts. Suggestion systems existed, but responses were rare, weak, and slow in coming. Many people had to evaluate suggestions and by the time approval was given the process might have already changed. There was very little contact between plant personnel and senior management. Every department functioned by itself and was responsible only for its own area of the business. There was almost no communication between departments and the result was a significant amount of waste. This is a classic example of a siloed company.

Companies believed that viable competition only existed within the United States. To strengthen its position, a company would make business decisions that were designed to hurt the competition in order to potentially drive them out of the marketplace. No consideration was given to the impact that moves like this could have on suppliers.

In the late 1960s and 1970s, more Asian companies entered the U.S. marketplace. The typical attitude within U.S. management was that their products were of lesser quality and they would not hurt our business. Remember the small portable radios from Japan? At first they were of poor quality, but the Japanese companies endeavored to try to improve their products and to be more competitive. Within a few years they became a major force in the electronics marketplace. Even today I see companies that still view their competition and market as only within the United States.

There was also arrogance among U.S. businesses that said "we are the best and no one can do this business better than us." A noteworthy example of this was the steel industry in Pittsburgh, Pennsylvania, in the early '80s. Everything was going along fine and then the foreign competition arrived. In self-defense, the Pittsburgh steel industry cried out for government protection, fines for dumping, and so on. In reality, the company had not focused on the business from a global perspective and was hurt badly by the competition that used new and cheaper technology in other countries. As a result, many steel mills were closed and many workers lost their jobs and had to find new careers.

These examples explain why many American industries fell behind Asia, and continue to face foreign competition. Today we can see the same scenario in the automobile industry. The Big Three (Ford, General Motors, and Chrysler) have been focused on the domestic car business and the foreign car companies have worked very hard to establish their businesses in the United States. The Big Three are operating on a cost basis and are seeking the lowest price anywhere in the world. In the meantime, their foreign competitors are working with local suppliers to produce quality parts at prices acceptable to the companies without constant pressure to reduce the price. The difference is apparent in that suppliers to the foreign automakers are not going bankrupt at the same rate as those for the Big Three. Today the domestic car companies have a major cash problem that compromises their ability to pay their bills in a timely manner. The result is that their suppliers in turn run out of money and have to file for Chapter 11 bankruptcy protection.

As you can see, the industry that focuses entirely on price may end up the loser in the long run if they do not watch what the competition is doing. Copying the foreign companies' procedures will not guarantee success either. The context of the process that you want to duplicate is important. Cultures in different countries have a major impact on how the processes actually perform. This will be discussed in more detail in Chapter 7, which addresses industry globalization.

The other concept that was very prevalent prior to the 1980s was the idea that if I lost a customer I would gain one from another company and it would all balance out in the end. As a result, there was no effort to earn customer loyalty. As the foreign companies arrived with their focus on customer needs and wants, customers that left the domestic producer often never returned to a domestic company. Quality and service were the keys to attracting and retaining customers. Both domestic and foreign companies realized this, but the foreign companies strived to achieve these and so gained greater results.

The business world continues to change, and each company must be ready to change with it, accepting new ideas in order to remain competitive in today's marketplace.

The model adopted in the 1960s can be depicted by two funnels with the small ends touching each other. These small ends represent the only point of interface between the customer and the supplier: sales on the supplier side and purchasing on the other (see Figure 1.1).

This model did not encourage the development of relationships between companies. It encouraged the development of friendships or at least business relationships between the salespeople from the supplier and the purchasing people from the customer. Most of the other people in both organizations had little if any contact with each other. To be an effective business today, this model must change. Companies need to be involved with each other at many deeper levels to reap the benefits of supply chain management.

Another concept that has been prevalent ever since the government bailed out Chrysler is that I don't have to be a careful manager because the government won't let an American company fail. Any newspaper today details the different demands businesses are making on the government for help. I believe that people have forgotten that the government has no money except what it takes from the citizens. Demanding that the government support businesses or any other private cause only spreads the burden to everyone. This will not solve U.S. industries' problems.

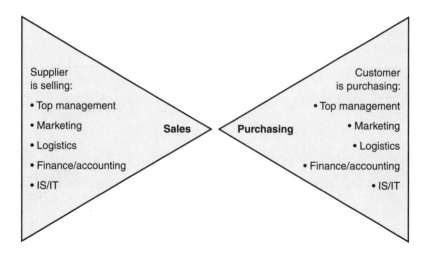

Figure 1.1 The old selling model.

Part of this misconception is not only that the government should take care of American companies but that companies should preserve jobs above profit. All companies are in business today to make a profit. When companies and employees get rid of entitlement attitudes and take responsibility for their own actions and attitudes we can make America a better place to do business.

Another policy that I still see promoted today is the concept of "Buy American." This is not a bad concept, but a recent article in the Sunday Detroit Free Press indicated that a Toyota car has about 80 percent of its parts manufactured in North America. Similar figures were presented for Honda. These two manufacturers are leading the industry. So if I buy a Toyota or a Honda vehicle, I am actually buying a primarily American-made vehicle. Does something seem wrong with this scenario? Shouldn't American companies be leading the automobile industry? As you can see, there is a deeper-rooted problem in U.S. industries than is immediately apparent. This has to change because American businesses need to become competitive on a global scale with our own products. Companies need to make the paradigm shifts rather than continue to rely on the government to rescue them.

CONCLUSION

The old philosophies of doing business are not going to work today. Changes need to happen. The question before us as individuals is, Are we willing to adapt even as the world changes?

KEYWORDS

Cost standards

Price

Old business model

DISCUSSION QUESTIONS

1. How have purchasing departments influenced procurement of raw materials?

2. Discuss an example of an organization that has been or is focused on the wrong customer.

3. How should a company and its management deal with the potential for local or national natural disasters?

4. Discuss a cost standard system that you are familiar with and the results that were obtained.

5. Why should a company or an individual change in today's world?

2

Understanding Your Supply Chain

L et's begin by defining what a *supply chain* is. It is the group of organizations and processes that a product goes through from its initial source (like an ore mine) to the finished product that is delivered to the customer. Depending on the product, this can be a very long chain and have many links in it.

A definition of the supply chain from the *APICS Dictionary,* Eighth Edition, 1995 is:

1) The processes from the initial raw materials to the ultimate consumption of the finished product linking across supplier–user companies.

2) The functions within and outside a company that enable the value chain to make products and provide services to the customer.

PROCESS MAPPING

This is one of the seven basic quality tools to help understand a process and then improve that process.

One definition of a process is a group of activities that together create value for the customer.

Using this definition there are a wide variety of different things that could be considered a process. This definition of a process is very appropriate for supply chain management. Many companies are involved in the process of getting a product to the consumer. There are several reasons that process mapping might be done. These are (a) quality assurance, (b) reengineering, (c) continuous improvement, (d) as a teaching tool. There are some specific terms related to process mapping that need to be explained. Different terms are used for different purposes in the process maps. Some of the terms that you will hear are: critical path, handoffs, waste, parallel processes, decision points, total cycle time, redundancy, exceptions (alternate routes), theoretical cycle time. All of these terms will have some application as we develop a supply chain map.

There are three types of process maps:

1. As-is (Now)

2. Could-be (Short-term goals have been included)

3. Should-be (Long-term goals have been included)

The last two types help the continuous improvement process as these maps are evaluated and then implemented.

Almost every department in an organization will use process mapping in some form, including sales, marketing, information technology, finance, project managers, quality, and others.

A process map is defined as a graphical representation of all the steps involved in an entire process.

Let's look at the steps in creating a process map.

1. Define the process steps. One of the ways to do this is to put a large sheet of brown shipping paper on the wall and have a group of people write down all of the steps that each one sees in the process being examined.

2. Sort the steps into the order of occurrence.

3. Place the steps in appropriate flowchart symbols.

4. Evaluate the steps for completeness, efficiency, and possible problems.

Let's look at an example of a process map. The situation is "buying gas for your car." What are the steps involved?

At a 50,000-foot level the process might look like Figure 2.1.

At a more detailed level, the process might look like Figure 2.2.

The next step in process mapping is to understand how your business operates and how the different departments interact with each other. This needs to be understood before you can begin to examine how the supply chain works and how improvements can be made. A process map for a business

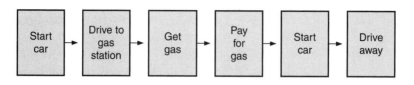

Figure 2.1   Process map for "buying gas for your car" at a very high (50,000-foot) level.

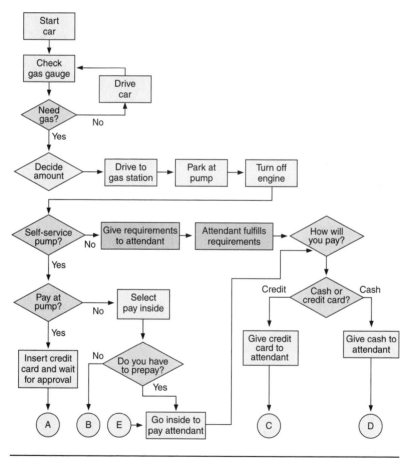

Figure 2.2   Process map for "buying gas for your car" at a much more detailed level.

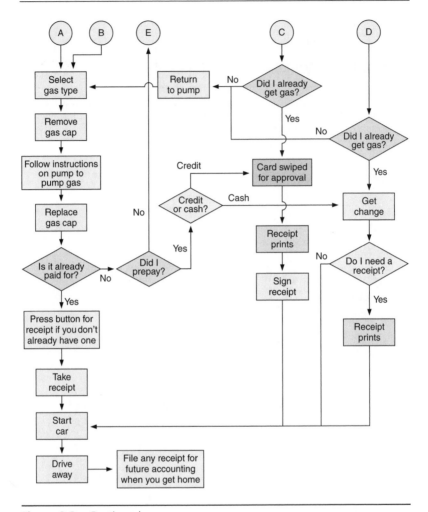

Figure 2.2 *Continued.*

may look like Figure 2.3. Its two maps cover an entire business. These process maps are created at a very detailed level for ease of understanding the business.

Now that you have an understanding of how your business operates, you can begin to look at the supply chain.

Using the quality tool of process mapping, a picture of the supply chain can be developed. When this process is started you must look at where the process begins and ends. This requires a good understanding of where your

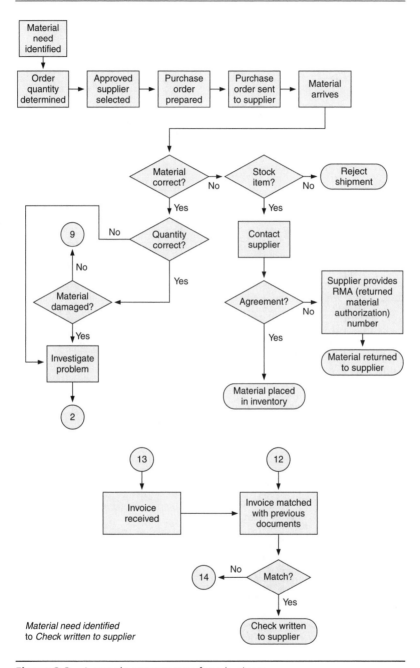

Figure 2.3   A sample process map for a business.

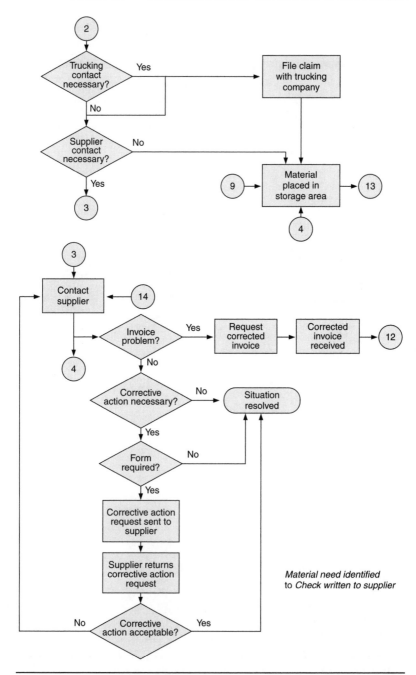

Figure 2.3   *Continued.*

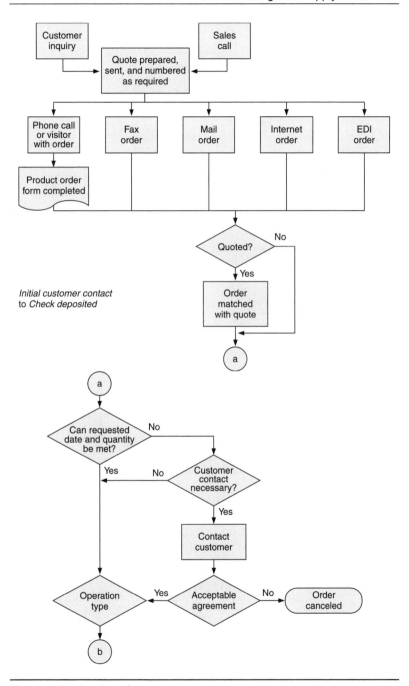

Figure 2.3   *Continued.*

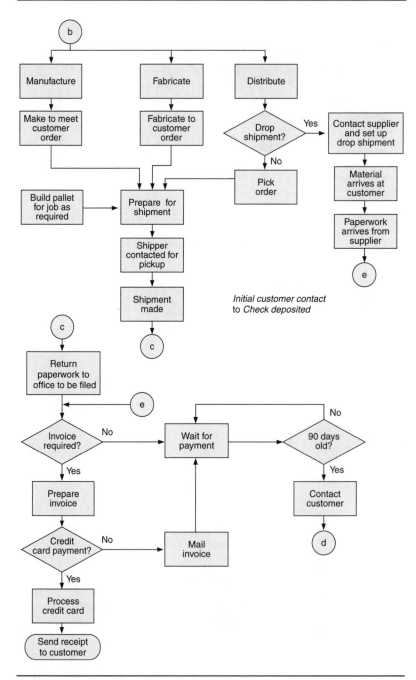

Figure 2.3   *Continued.*

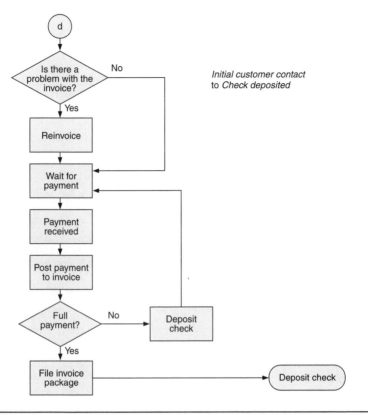

Figure 2.3 *Continued.*

finished product is used and what the consumer finally sees. Many times the folks in the sales and marketing areas can be called on to help fill in some of the organizations and processes on the upstream side of the supply chain. The downstream side of the chain can be supplied by the purchasing department and knowledge gained from suppliers. By going through a process like this, a much clearer understanding of your business is developed as well as where it fits in the supply chain and what economic factors really influence your business.

The beginning point for this process is to list your raw materials and then your finished products. These are your inputs and outputs. The finished products are followed until they reach the consumer, while the raw materials are followed to their initial source. This should be completed at a very high level at first just to get a basic understanding of what is involved. Once the high-level list is complete a more detailed one can be prepared as needed by the organization. See Table 2.1.

Table 2.1 Four examples of raw materials and finished products.

Example one

Raw materials	Finished products
Mixed cresols	Di-butyl para cresol (BHT)
Isobutylene	
Acid catalyst	
Caustic soda	
Crystallization solvent	
Paper bag	

Example two

Raw materials	Finished products
Deionized water	Cleaning product (dishwashing soap, hand cleaning soap, and so on)
Surfactants	
Dyes	
Fragrances	
Bottles	
Cardboard cases	

Example three

Raw materials	Finished products
Coal	Coke
	Coke gas
	Coal tar

Example four

Raw materials	Finished products
Steel	Steel stamping
Cutting oils	

The next step in the process is to begin to develop the map of the supply chain for your organization.

Several examples of maps of different supply chains are shown here. Figure 2.4 is a general supply chain map. It shows the basic model of the supply chain and all the elements that need to be included. From this

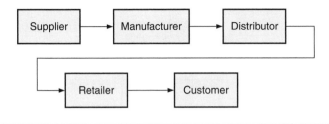

Figure 2.4   General supply chain map.

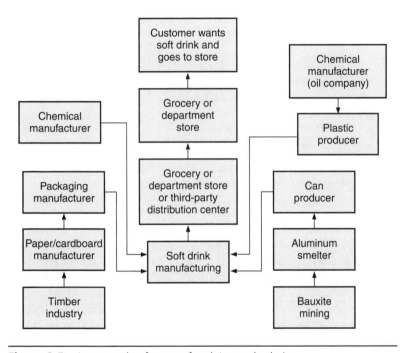

Figure 2.5   An example of a can of soda's supply chain.

process map and Table 2.1 you can begin to develop a map for your business. Some specific examples are shown in Figures 2.5 and 2.6.

It is important to understand where your organization fits into the supply chain; then you can begin to see the impact that other customers and suppliers can have on your business. An example of this would be in the mid '90s when General Suharto, the President of Indonesia, ruled that no more palm kernel oil could be exported from this country. Indonesia at

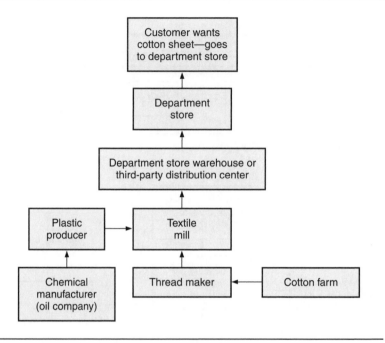

Figure 2.6   An example of a cotton sheet's supply chain.

the time provided nearly 70 percent of the world's supply. Since palm kernel oil is one of the raw materials used in the manufacture of surfactants for cleaning products, there was an immediate need for a different substance to be used as a raw material. Companies had to make changes rapidly so that the market share for their products did not decline. As you can see, by understanding your supply chain you will get an indication of how near to the source and final consumer you are, and you may be able to see where possible interruptions could occur.

The next step to take is to look at where the costs of the supply chain are incurred in your part of the chain. Are you located near your major suppliers or are they far away? Do you use just-in-time deliveries? These are some of the questions that should be asked. Some of the categories of costs that occur in the supply chain are:

- *Acquisition costs.* These are costs incurred during the process of obtaining the necessary materials or services.

- *Possession costs.* These are the costs incurred while the material is being stored and/or being used.

- *Application costs.* These are costs incurred during the manufacturing of the product or the delivery of the service.

- *Inspection costs.* These are costs incurred while performing the required inspections.

- *Internal/external failure costs.* These are costs incurred because of failures that are identified before they reach the customer and failures that have reached the customer.

These five areas cover the costs that can be incurred throughout the entire supply chain within each organization that is involved. This detail was provided by the authors of *Supercharging Supply Chains*.

Let's look at each of these costs in more detail.

ACQUISITION COSTS

The Labor to Process Purchase Orders

It costs companies in excess of $100 to process a single purchase order. This is a cost that can easily be overlooked when evaluations are being completed. Taking this into consideration is one way to make sure that the purchasing area gets accurately reflected in the costs. It is easy just to consider this cost as overhead but when it is handled that way the real opportunities for improvement may be hidden. Some companies today are developing processes that are all-electronic, eliminating the paper purchase order process. The Big Three U.S. auto companies are now taking advantage of the Internet and posting their requirements on a Web site and expecting their suppliers to check the site and deliver to those requirements. As a result, no purchase orders are being produced and a cost savings is resulting for many businesses.

Computers to Prepare, Track, and Verify Orders and Shipments

Larger companies today are moving toward requiring a bar code on raw materials that is scanned when the material arrives. This is automatically matched with the purchase order and the material is marked in the system as received, and in the more sophisticated systems an electronic payment is issued for the goods received. As you can see, there can be a large investment required to make all of these processes happen. Radio frequency readers are also being used to identify products at various stages in the supply chain. More and more software applications are being developed that should make these processes more efficient and better able to help the supply chain to improve. Some examples of software packages are: MRP (materials requirements planning), ERP (enterprise resource planning), CRM (customer relationship management), and various forecasting software applications. All of these are designed to help companies understand their businesses and make better decisions.

Labor to Expedite Late Deliveries

This is a process of tracking an order to try to find out where it is and when it can be expected to arrive at your facility. In order to reduce some of the costs at FedEx and UPS, tracking systems have been developed and made available to their customers so they are able to track their own packages when they need to and not rely on the customer service department at the shipping company. This has improved service and helped satisfy their customers much faster and better. I have observed companies that have entire departments whose responsibility is to follow shipments and expedite them as necessary so everything runs as planned. This is a potentially expensive area that can be handled more effectively with proper supply chain management.

Building and Office Space

Office space can be rented or owned but there are costs involved in both. Buildings are rented by the square foot and can be charged to the various departments in the same way whether rented or owned. Office space and building space are assets but can be very expensive to have. A balance between size and the ability to get the jobs accomplished needs to be developed when building sizes are determined.

An example of a space issue is when engineering is asked to double the capacity of an operation. The easy way to do this is to duplicate what already exists. When this is done the inefficiencies of the existing process are carried on to the new operation. The entire process needs to be evaluated and new technology needs to be considered, as well as what changes can be made to the existing operation to increase capacity. I have seen an operation that was producing as much as 25 to 30 percent scrap that was not even being measured. As process changes were made to reduce the scrap, a planned addition to the plant was not needed. In this case a small investment changed the process and increased the needed capacity, rather than a large capital expenditure.

Supervision of Sourcing Process

The head of the purchasing department must oversee the entire process and make sure that it is following the requirements of the organization. A good portion of the leader's time would be spent in this area of supervision. Staff must be trained in the requirements of the organization and boundaries need to be set as to what they are able to change. Once a sourcing decision is made, everyone in the organization should follow the decision as it is communicated throughout the organization.

Labor to Prepare and Process Multiple Bids on Low-Value Items

Many companies and organizations require three bids to be able to make a purchasing decision. This costs the supplier in preparation and the purchaser in the effort of evaluating and deciding which bid best fits the needs of the organization. This is where the companies' requirements need to be specifically defined. The thing to remember when getting bids is, what are your criteria for selecting the bid? You must be aware if you are using price alone that you may have bids that will cut corners. Price is negotiable and you must first make sure that the specified requirements are being met. If a company is trying to get business they may lowball a job to try to force their way into an organization. Falling for this may cause problems later as more money will have to be spent correcting problems.

POSSESSION COSTS

Operating and Depreciating Inventory-Holding Space

Space is expensive. The larger the inventory, the more money the space will require. The larger the inventory, the greater the risk of having products go obsolete. Inventory ties up working capital that then can not be used to effectively run the business.

Heat and Other Utilities

Buildings have to be heated, cooled, and have electricity and water. Many companies have separate meters for the offices and the production areas to help separate the costs. Depending on the climate this can be a significant expense for the business.

Janitorial and Guard Personnel

These are the personnel that keep the facilities safe and secure as well as clean. I have seen these services contracted as well as performed by employees of the organization. This depends on the management strategy of the organization.

Routine and Special Building Maintenance and Repair

Buildings require maintenance like roof repairs, overhead doors fixed, and so on. These charges have typically shown up as overhead charges. As I said before, care needs to be taken in what gets defined as overhead so that real costs do not get ignored or masked by other charges.

Taxes on Land, Building, and Inventory

This is a nonoperating cost and is a function of the state and municipality in which the facilities are located. If you have a plant that crosses boundaries between two municipalities you may have to meet the requirements of both municipalities. Most states now have a tax on goods sold and inventories. This also will vary depending on the location. This is where the tax breaks for companies to locate in an area are often given.

Insurance on Building and Equipment

There are many different types of insurance that need to be considered. Some examples are: business interruption, machine replacement, building replacement, and so on. Again, this is a nonoperating cost and is a function of value, which is driven by space.

Liability Insurance

Liability insurance is needed to protect the business if someone is hurt while working, someone is injured on the property, and so on. Workers compensation is part of this and covers an employee's wages while they are away from work.

Yearly Interest on Loans Made to Purchase MRO Items

Maintenance, repair, and operating (MRO) supplies are needed to run a business and these require cash to cover their costs. If working capital gets low, loans are taken to get the needed cash. The interest rate may vary but will continue to exist until the loan is paid off.

Estimated Loss of Return on Inventory Capital

Shrinkage is a term for lost or damaged material that occurs while material is in inventory. Any loss or scrapped material is a loss of value from the investments in the inventory and thus will not be able to return the value or investment.

Average Yearly Loss from Materials Obsolescence and Pilferage

These are problems that exist in large inventories. Employees think that something won't be missed if there is a large quantity. If engineering drawings are involved, changes can come along and make an entire stock of material obsolete. Depending on the relationship with the customer, this may be a shared cost or the customer might use up the old stock first. I have observed some companies that say to the supplier, "The stock is yours and you have to figure out what you will do with it." This does not create healthy suppliers or good relationships.

In-Plant Damage or Deterioration

Much in-plant damage can be caused by forklifts. They are a great way to move material around, but they can cause damage by running over things as well as hitting drums, bags, or other pallets with the forks. Another concern is when you are dealing with steel products; they can rust if they are held in inventory for an extended period of time, requiring a cleaning process before they can be shipped. Parts that are dropped may or may not be acceptable at the next operation. This is another area where the scrap measurement would give an indication of what is happening in the operation.

Labor to Receive, Stock, Identify, Move, and Maintain Materials

This has been defined in many organizations as receiving inspection or just receiving. Normally this is handled by a group of people for whom this is their only responsibility.

Extra Accounting Hours Necessitated for Inventory Control

When a physical inventory is completed and matched with the inventory that exists on the books, adjustments have to be made and accounting has to handle all of the adjustments as well as calculate the costs involved.

Supervisory Cost of Inventory

This is normally handled by a warehouse supervisor. The responsibility of this supervisor is to manage the warehouse and make sure that the necessary shipments are being made as well as fulfill the material movement requirements within the operations.

Top Management Time Spent Solving Inventory Problems

When the inventory gets out of control, top management must be involved to make the decision as to how the inventory will be dealt with. Top management will have to make the decision to take a large write-off or not and determine how they will correct what happened to cause the issue at hand.

APPLICATION COSTS

Labor to Engineer and Specify Products for New Applications

As processes change, engineering is required to rewrite the specifications for the new equipment or raw materials for the production process. Research and development is probably the department that came up with the new application and engineering has to do the scale-up to manufacturing size. Sometimes when new applications are developed, the research group uses the purest laboratory-grade materials that are available. These materials may not even be available in the volumes required for production and are probably not cost-effective. Research should also be completed with the commercially available materials. This will give a good idea of any problems that might be encountered in manufacturing.

Labor to Upgrade Products for More Efficient Operation

This labor again is probably in research and development or engineering. For example, in the automotive industry this would be an engineering change to make the part function better or fit in its location better.

Downtime Due to Wrong Products

This can be due to supplier shipping the wrong materials or because the operation is set up for the wrong or a different product. Downtime can cause problems for customers as it creates a potential capacity problem in your operations, which may be able to be covered with overtime but will raise costs.

Training Personnel to Use Products

Sales personnel need to be trained on the application of products and how and where they can be used. An example that I have seen in this area is a cleaning products manufacturer who had to train the sales force on what each of their cleaners would do and where they could effectively be used. This company had a variety of different applications and had developed training for each application.

INSPECTION COSTS

Labor to Investigate and Conduct Inspection

Inspectors are laborers. They inspect materials based on approved criteria and determine if the material is good or bad.

Material and Storage Costs Associated with Inspection

Material that is being inspected requires floor space in which to store it before it moves on to the next operation. Companies sometimes have inspection/storage points right on the production line.

Special Equipment and/or Procedure for Inspections

The gages or instruments used must be able to measure the critical dimensions or characteristics of the material. One client used a coordinate measurement machine (CMM) to validate all measurements on the final products. Micrometers and calipers are used as in-process gages but the CMM is used to get the final result.

INTERNAL/EXTERNAL FAILURE COSTS

Line Pulls and Associated Failures. If an internal failure occurs, the line is stopped and the problem is resolved. This causes downtime and associated problems with getting the correct parts or correcting the problems that have been encountered.

Warranty Costs. These costs can be a major expense and in many cases they are not really monitored. The cost systems that exist in many organizations do not have the capability to tie warranty costs back to the parts, the supplier, and the buyer. In the automobile industry this cost becomes very large as the warranties get extended.

Rework/Scrap Costs. Scrap and rework can consume significant amounts of labor in trying to recover the material. Scrap recovery savings are always less than the cost of the original material. This is a good candidate for continuous improvement, and I have seen a lot of low-hanging fruit to be picked in the area of scrap reduction.

Impositions on Bottleneck Operations. If a process is a bottleneck, it will cause capacity problems as well as scheduling issues. The concept of synchronous manufacturing needs to be implemented along with work on reducing inventories. Bottlenecks need to be removed so that processes can run smoothly.

As you consider changes to your organization and its supply base, the first area that needs to be looked at is the decision whether you will make a product or whether you will buy that product. This is the first decision that is involved in the supply chain management process. Chapter 4 will deal with this topic in detail.

The ultimate driver in supply chain management is the consumer. This is the person who sees enough value in the product to be willing to spend some of his or her hard-earned money to purchase it. As part of supply chain management we need to be constantly aware of the changing needs of the consumer.

How do we discover these changing needs? Part of this is done by market research firms. Surveys and testing give indications of the changes that are happening and what product changes may or may not be accepted in the market. Supply chain management strategy will be discussed in detail in Chapter 3.

This process is a little different in the automobile industry. New features are developed by engineers that add to the features of existing automobiles, and then a concept car is made and displayed at various auto shows around the world. Interest and reactions are measured at these shows to determine which features should be added and which ones should be dropped.

In the marketplace today, one of the critical pieces in the supply chain is flexibility. Consumers' needs change based on global economic situations. An example of this is how difficulties in the Middle East have caused the price of gasoline to rise. Many consumers are now looking for vehicles that are multi-fuel or have higher miles-per-gallon ratings. Unfortunately, the U.S. Big Three (General Motors, Ford, and Chrysler) automakers designed and built many plants to manufacture one type of vehicle only. The equipment has no flexibility other than to produce one type of vehicle.

The transplant companies on the other hand have designed flexibility into their facilities. One assembly plant is capable of assembling the company's entire product line on-site. Operating in this manner requires a very strong supply chain management process to make sure all the parts are at the right place at the right time. This also allows the plant to do their forecasting and production closer to the actual consumers' demand. This type of operation reduces the amount of inventory required as well as all the working capital that is usually tied up in inventories.

One of the newer positions that has been created is the *supplier quality engineer*. These "engineers" are given the responsibility of working with the suppliers to get the products that are required. In many cases I have seen individuals in these positions go on an ego trip and try to show how powerful they are. Many of them do not understand the impact that their actions can have on the overall business. To illustrate this let me use an example:

A large company gets a new vice president of purchasing who wants to make a name for himself quickly. His predecessor had been squeezing the suppliers to reduce costs for five years. The new vice president wants all existing contracts torn up and rebid to get lower prices. The contracts are all awarded to the suppliers based on the lowest price alone. As a result, in the short term the new vice president saves the company a tremendous amount of money and he really impresses the board of directors.

Now let's analyze the supply chain impacts of this move.

Many of the contracts were moved to different suppliers so there was a lot of shifting of business in the supply chain. This shifting created negative responses in many organizations in the supply chain.

What might happen at the end of these contracts? If I were one of the suppliers that had been replaced, would I bother to bid for the business again? If I did I would make sure I made good money. If one of the selected suppliers had financial problems, would I help the customer out? Maybe. How bad did the business get hurt in the long run by these price decisions? As a result of situations like this, I have seen suppliers change focus and move on without this business.

The real issue when dealing with the supply chain in this manner is that it is very easy to end up with unhealthy suppliers in the financial sense. What do you do if a supplier files for Chapter 11 bankruptcy? How does this impact your business? What happens if the supplier gets closed down or files for Chapter 7 bankruptcy?

I saw a situation where the bank closed down a business because they ran out of credit. Part of this was caused by members in the supply chain not paying their bills in a timely manner. The company was toward the beginning of the supply chain so many downstream organizations suffered as a result of this move. This is hard to predict, so each company needs to be aware of the status of their supplier's financial health.

All of this said, the need exists for supply chain managers in any and all businesses. The real questions become "How are we as a company going to do it?" and "What kind of relationships are we going to have with our suppliers?" Both of these questions have multiple ways of being answered but the best for each situation has to be developed. One of the difficulties that exists is that this process of supply chain management is different for every part of the supply chain. Each part needs to be evaluated and decisions made as to what should be done.

Many companies think that long-term contracts are what drive supplier relationships. As a result they make sure that there is lots of legalese in the contracts to protect them as the customer. Does this work? Not eally! I have seen steel manufacturers and distributors that had contracts ith suppliers to get materials. These should be met, but with the global steel shortage in the first part of 2006 many distributors were unable to get any steel. The customers of the distributors sued in some cases for breach of contract but it only caused the destruction of the distributor and got them no steel. We have to understand the supply chain on a global basis so that the correct decisions are made and our business can obtain the material that we need to continue to operate.

THINGS THAT ARE BEYOND OUR CONTROL IN THE SUPPLY CHAIN

Consider the zebra mussel's invasion of the Great Lakes. These little crustaceans got into the Great Lakes and began to multiply. Today if you go to a beach along Lake Erie you will see piles of shells along the shore. These creatures move about as they attach themselves to ships and other seacraft and are carried into new areas. They cause water intakes at manufacturing or other facilities to plug, causing many associated problems. These issues were not anticipated when zebra mussels first arrived and many problems had to be fixed to keep plants running. Now companies are aware of the problem and are able to deal with this in the design stages. The entire supply chain was affected by this as companies had plants shut down for repairs while the inlets were being cleaned. Unless there is enough product in inventory, other plants in the supply chain could also be shut down.

Another example is palm kernel oil in Indonesia. In order to attempt to protect the economy of Indonesia a few years ago, General Suharto banned the export of all palm kernel oil from Indonesia, eliminating 70 percent of the world's supply. This created an immediate market shortage that impacted many product lines around the world. Much of this material was being purchased on long-term contracts that essentially became null and void when this happened.

Again, an entire supply chain was impacted by a decision that was made by a leader of a foreign land. This is an example of how we need to be aware of many of the things that are happening around the world. There are many good resources for this and they need to be used. One of the easiest ones is the front page of the *Wall Street Journal*. This has very short paragraphs about changes that are happening in countries around the world. If you are doing business in these countries or they are involved in your supply chain, you can also read the full story.

Many contracts have *force majeure* clauses in them that break the contract in event of some sort of catastrophe that can immediately impact the supply chain. Some examples of this are: a fire in a chemical plant, a hurricane like Katrina, a tornado, or earthquake. If you have a good relationship with the supplier, you will find out about this sooner than if you do not have a good relationship.

I was in a situation where the company I was dealing with had a major breakdown and could not meet their contract demands so they had to declare *force majeure* to protect the company. Some customers were not happy about this, but they had to deal with it.

Several other companies that I have been involved with over the years have had to use this clause in their contract. They had a natural disaster, fire, explosion, and so on, that caused their production capability to cease indefinitely.

Global Supply Impact

As more and more companies are dealing with Asian countries, the supply chains become vulnerable to a ship sinking with your container on it. It may be insured to cover losses, but what happens to your production while the next container gets manufactured and shipped and travels to your business?

Credit Line of Supplier Runs Out

This is an area where the complete supply chain must be understood. You must understand the material flow, but you should also understand the flow of money. A supplier in your supply chain several levels upstream can run out of cash due to a long time being taken by a customer to pay bills. When the credit line that is available is used up, the only option the supplier may have is to shut down until a payment is received. A move like this can cause an entire supply chain to stop or shut down.

CONCLUSION

We have just looked at the two most important process maps for a supply chain. The first one was the internal one for your business that shows all of the interfaces that exist within your organization. This process map shows where any opportunities for improvement might exist. The second map shows the linkages between different companies and how they all work together to produce and get a product to the consumer. Once you understand your supply chain, you are now able to begin to proceed to the development of a supply chain management strategy. Supply chains can be impacted by events that are beyond the absolute control of the supply chain members. A complete risk analysis needs to be completed to understand what impact some external events might have on the supply chain and the customer.

KEYWORDS

Process mapping

Supply chain management

Supply chain map

Acquisition costs

Possession costs

Application costs

Inspection costs

Internal/external failure costs

DISCUSSION QUESTIONS

1. Define a supply chain.

2. What types of costs are involved in a business?

3. Develop a map of the supply chain for your organization. Did you identify any weak links in the process? What were they?

4. Make a process map for the process of preparing pancakes for breakfast.

5. What are some things that can happen in other businesses that can have an impact on your business? What are the plans to deal with these?

6. Read the local newspaper and find an article that describes an international happening. Discuss how this event might have an impact on supply chains of organizations.

3

Developing a Supply Chain Management Strategy

WHERE DOES SUPPLY CHAIN MANAGEMENT FIT INTO THE MISSION AND VISION OF AN ORGANIZATION?

Supply chain management has to be a part of the strategy of the organization. What does this mean? The top executives need to make this a part of the strategy and strategic plan of the organization. What types of relationships and actions will be handled by the organization and how far down the supply chain the organization will be involved need to be defined and supported by the strategic plan.

In many organizations the complete strategic plan is not available to many of the employees so the commitment of the top management personnel must be visible to the employees in the vision and mission statements as well as the goals and objectives. Examples can be observed by searching various Web sites for mission, vision, and values statements of corporations that interest you personally.

There are many areas that need to be covered in the mission statement specifically. One of these is the relationship with customers and suppliers. By placing this in the mission statement it is easy to communicate the executive commitment to managing the supply chain. Effective supply chain management really is based on relationships.

SUPPLY CHAIN MANAGEMENT MATURITY MODEL

A five-level model that can be used to evaluate where a company is in the handling of supply chain management has been developed. Each of the levels describes different customer–supplier situations. I am suggesting a five-level model that is similar to other types of maturity models that may be used for project management, information technology, and so on. As shown in Figure 3.1, the stages in the model are:

Level one. Individual company's departments functioning independently with no or very little interaction with customers or suppliers. This is a siloed company.

Level two. Internal company integration of departments. The organization is functioning as a unit instead of siloed departments.

Level three. One level of integration. Relationships are being built with either customers or suppliers and the companies are working together for the common good of both organizations.

Level four. Two levels of integration. Relationships are being built with both customers and suppliers and these companies are working together for the benefit of all three organizations. At least three or four organizations are involved in the process.

Level five. Entire supply chain integration. This is where a supply chain from the initial raw material to the consumer is integrated and working together for the benefit of the entire supply chain. Many more organizations are working together for the benefit of each other.

See Figure 3.2 for a summary graphic of this model.

Supply chain management is a specialized form of strategic management. It must become a major part of business strategy. Supply chain management is the area of management that will attempt to be sure that the customer's needs will be able to be met and you will have a reason to be in business.

The supply chain management strategy should be covered in the large umbrella of the vision statement for the organization.

A company may choose to have a separate mission statement for the supply chain. This mission statement should include:

1. *Customers.* Some of the questions that need to be considered as this area of the mission statement is developed are:

   a. How are customers viewed by the organization?

   b. How important is our business to this customer?

   c. What type of relationship do we want to have with the customers?

   d. How are the customers going to be monitored?

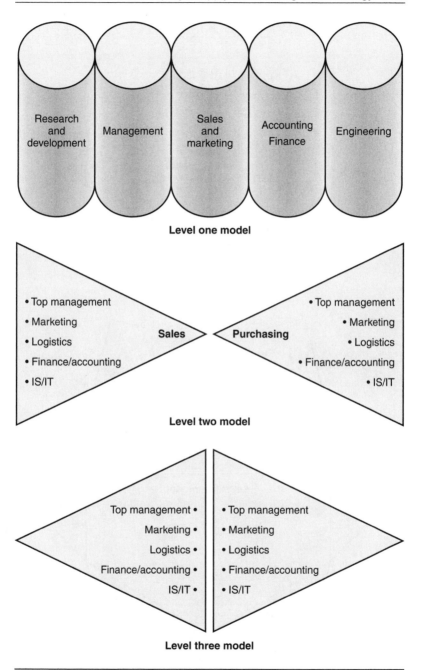

Figure 3.1   A five-level model to evaluate where a company is in the handling of supply chain management.

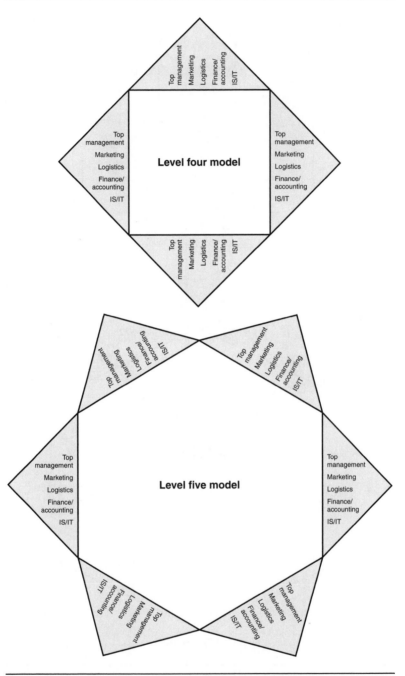

Figure 3.1 Continued.

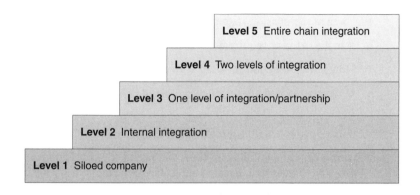

Figure 3.2   Supply chain maturity model.

2. *Suppliers.* Some of the questions that need to be considered as this area of the mission statement is developed are:

   a. What type of relationship will the organization have with the supplier?

   b. How will the supplier be monitored and rewarded?

   c. How are suppliers viewed by the organization?

   d. How will the supplier's business impact this organization's business?

   e. How are suppliers identified and selected?

3. *Quality.* Some of the questions that need to be considered as this area of the mission statement is developed are:

   a. What measures might be used for quality for the customer and from the supplier?

   b. How will continuous improvement happen in this supply chain?

   c. Who will be involved in the decision-making process?

   d. Are the requirements clear to the supplier and is the supplier capable?

   e. Am I causing extra processing to be done by the supplier that I really do not need?

4. *Delivery.* Some of the questions that need to be considered as this area of the mission statement is developed are:

   a. Are the delivery requirements made clear to the supplier?

   b. How will interactions dealing with deliveries be handled?

   c. Will there be penalties for late or missed deliveries? How will these be handled?

   d. What are the benefits of early deliveries?

5. *Environment.* Some of the questions that need to be considered as this area of the mission statement is developed are:

   a. How does this company deal with environmental issues and what are your expectations?

   b. Are the environmental expectations communicated to the supplier clearly?

   c. Will a supplier be penalized for environmental issues?

6. *Employees.* Some of the questions that need to be considered as this area of the mission statement is developed are:

   a. How will employees interact with members of the supply chain?

   b. What responsibility and authority will the employees have?

   c. Will the supplier's employees be empowered the same way?

   d. Are the expectations communicated clearly to the employees?

HOW ARE NEEDS FORECASTED?

Many companies rely on the sales and marketing departments to provide the forecasts of the material needs for the next period. In my experience I have found both of these groups to be very optimistic in their projections. When this happens the extra materials have to be stored in inventory.

One solution for this is to build the forecasts from demand data that is obtained from the consumer. Many retail stores now have scanning devices that generate point-of-sale data. This produces actual sales figures for each piece of merchandise. This information needs to make it to the manufacturer so that it can be used to project production levels. This is the ideal situation and is what happens in a pull system. A pull system is driven by actual demand. As an order is placed (creating demand) the material ordered is made for the customer. One of the main benefits of a pull system is a major reduction of the work-in-process (WIP) inventory.

As inventory is maintained at various warehouses as well as the manufacturer, a large amount of material can be sitting in inventory in the supply chain. As replacement orders pass down the supply chain, the orders are pulled from the inventory that is available. If we look at a simple example of a retail store to a warehouse to the manufacturer, the order quantities will be smaller from the retail store to the warehouse, which will try to cover the orders quickly with inventory. When the inventory reaches a low level at the warehouse, a larger replacement order is placed with the manufacturer. The retail store may order 10 items per week, and the warehouse has an inventory of 100 items. For nine weeks there are no orders placed to the manufacturer and in the tenth week an order for 100 items is placed. If the manufacturer had 100 items in inventory they would have been held for more than nine weeks before they could be shipped to the customer. This adds storage costs to the manufacturer and can disrupt the production schedule when the large order arrives. This reaction in the supply chain is called the "bullwhip effect."

In order to overcome the bullwhip effect in the supply chain, better forecasting techniques need to be used to predict the demand for the material for the next period as the production schedules are produced.

Forecasting Techniques

There are a variety of forecasting techniques available. The technique that will work best for the organization is one that must be determined by the cost of the forecast preparation and the accuracy that is required. There needs to be a cost justification between these two areas so that the best results are obtained.

Some examples of various forecasting methods that can be used are:

- *Naïve.* These methods assume that recent periods are the best predictors of the future. Therefore the actual for the current period becomes the forecast for the next period.

- *Moving average.* These methods try to eliminate randomness in a time series and smooth the curve of the data. This method of forecasting tends to lag a trend, and the more periods included in the average, the greater the lag will be. This method is best suited for products that have a stable demand.

- *Exponential smoothing.* These methods are similar to moving average methods but values are weighted exponentially, giving more weight to the most recent data. This forecasting method works well when dealing with stable items. It is good for short-range forecasts but not the best choice for low or intermittent demand situations.

- *Linear regression.* These methods assume a cause-and-effect relationship between the input to a system and its output.

- *Multiple regression.* These methods assume a cause-and-effect relationship between more than one input to a system and its output.

These are the five basic techniques that can be used. There have been several special models developed for special cases. A few examples of these are:

- Brown's exponential smoothing method is used for forecasting time series data that have a linear trend. This method is similar to double moving average techniques. Only one smoothing constant is used in this method.

- Holt's two-parameter linear-exponential smoothing method is used to smooth trend and slope directly by using different smoothing constants for each. Using two constants gives more flexibility in selecting rates at which trend and slope can be followed.

- Gompertz growth curves can be used to represent the tendency of many products and industries to grow at a declining rate as they reach maturity.

- Winter's three-parameter linear and seasonal exponential smoothing model is an extension of Holt's method to cover seasonal variation. This method uses a seasonal index to estimate seasonality.

- Autoregressive moving average (ARMA) models, also known as Box-Jenkins methods, combine the strengths of both the autoregressive and the moving average methods without assumptions about the number of terms in the forecast equation or the interrelationships of the coefficients.

Each of the above models has been developed to handle a specific form of variation in the data. Supply chain data would fall into the time series category where the reference point is a function of time. Production forecasts are completed monthly and broken down further as necessary. The longer the forecast time the greater the possibility of inaccuracy.

There are four parts of a forecast that need to be considered. These are:

- Is there a trend in the data?

- Are there changes due to the seasons?

- Is there a business cycle going on?

- Has or will an irregular event happen? (Hurricane, flood, strike, explosion, and so on)

By gaining an understanding of these four parts of the data, a model/technique can be selected and used that will satisfy the cost and accuracy measurements that are required for the forecast.

For more information on forecasting you can refer to a forecasting text or a statistics book.

HOW MUCH AND WHAT TYPES OF RISKS CAN BE ACCEPTED?

Every organization has risks and has a level of risk that they are willing to accept. This is an area that needs to be shared between customers and suppliers so that an understanding of what could happen to each one is clear.

An example of this would be a supplier that had one delivery truck and its maintenance was handled by a contractor. This supplier was willing to risk that a shipment would not be delivered because of a breakdown of the delivery truck. From the customer's perspective, a lack of material may shut their plant down and a backup vehicle may be necessary to guarantee that material is delivered, otherwise a larger inventory would have to be maintained to cover a time when the delivery truck was down. This shows that the supplier was willing to accept the risk of a truck breakdown and have the contractor repair it while the customer had to implement actions that would guarantee that material would always be there for the production to run.

The potential for catastrophic events dictates a need to have plans in place to keep the supply chain functioning. This may involve developing an alternate source if production is interrupted.

HOW WILL COMPETITIVE ADVANTAGE BE DEVELOPED?

Porter has written several books on competitive advantage. He has some very good concepts that can be used. There are several different strategies that can be used to create competitive advantage. These are:

- *Forward integration.* More control is obtained of distributors or even retailers.

- *Backward integration.* More control is obtained over suppliers.

- *Horizontal integration.* More control is obtained over competitors.

- *Market penetration.* More market share is obtained for existing products through marketing efforts.

- *Market development.* Current products are introduced into a new market.

- *Product development.* Current products are improved to better service the market or develop new products.

- *Concentric diversification.* New products are added but they are related to the current ones.

- *Conglomerate diversification.* New products are added and they are unrelated to the current ones.

- *Horizontal diversification.* New and unrelated products are added for current customers.

- *Retrenchment.* Regrouping is being done to reverse declining sales and profits.

- *Divestiture.* Part of an organization may be sold.

- *Liquidation.* All of the tangible assets of the organization are sold.

These are the different strategies that can be implemented in an organization. As one or more of these strategies are selected, the impact on the supply chain must be considered. Let's look at each one for their impact on the supply chain.

Forward Integration

This strategy can change the relationship with the customer. As a result, new and/or different types of relationships will be involved. A new supply chain map will need to be developed and the necessary changes required will have to be understood and communicated to the organization for this strategy to be successful.

Backward Integration

This strategy will change the relationship with a supplier. Again, different types of relationships will need to be developed. As a new map of the supply chain is completed and understood, the new requirements need to be communicated to the organization for this strategy to be successful.

Horizontal Integration

This strategy involves competitors and may increase customers as well as the requirements from suppliers. This is a way to attempt to obtain more market share and increase the top-line revenue for an organization. New customers will have to have relationships built while the suppliers may be able to function with the existing relationships. This strategy may involve merger or acquisition, and top management will need to deal with the integration of the two companies into one to be able to have a successful strategy.

Market Penetration

This strategy involves advertising products to the same customers and maybe even offering discounts to purchase your products. An example of this recently was the rebates that were offered in the auto industry to encourage people to buy cars. Each week we get ads in the mail for sales and these are an attempt by companies to increase market penetration by encouraging people to buy from them. This can be a very costly strategy depending on the form of advertising that is used and the gains that are actually received.

Market Development

This strategy is successful when a company uses creativity with their products and applies them to other areas or businesses. An example of this is where polyester resins are the basis for many different things like shower stalls, bowling balls, shirt buttons, car parts, boats, and so on. Creativity was used when each of these markets was opened. Top management needs to allow their people to be creative so that this strategy can be successful.

Product Development

This strategy works well when existing products are improved so that they perform better than the competitor's product or a new product is developed that creates a new or better market. This strategy may require that new supply chains be developed and new relationships be built. This strategy is much like starting from the beginning in many cases and the opportunity is there to do a great job at establishing proper supply chain management.

Concentric Diversification

This strategy helps a company expand their existing product line with related types of products so they are better able to support their customers. The supply chain in this strategy will be very much the same so that relationships may be built upon and expanded. A few new relationships may have to be built but most of the suppliers will already be in place.

Conglomerate Diversification

As this strategy is implemented new supply chains may have to be developed for unrelated products. Each supply chain requires a form of management and each supply chain has a critical supplier in it. This supplier needs to be identified, and the relationships that will be required must be developed. If the diversification is accomplished by a merger or acquisition, the supply chain may have to be adjusted to the arrangements used by the acquiring company. Many times there are new suppliers and customers involved in this type of diversification so the supply chain will grow substantially if it is not managed.

Horizontal Diversification

This strategy looks at the customer's needs and tries to fulfill them with your company's products. This is a good strategy if you have related products that can be used in different operations. In this case the supply chain would just receive an increase in volume and all of the players in the chain would already be in place. This strategy works very well in an industry like commercial cleaning products where an entire line of products is already being manufactured.

Retrenchment

This strategy involves shrinking the supply chain as products and even businesses are removed. Consideration of the suppliers' capabilities has to happen so that the supplier is able to remain in business. If this situation is handled poorly, a supplier for many different materials may be lost. A company's main or critical products need to be protected by healthy suppliers.

Divestiture

This strategy involves removing portions of the supply chain. The remaining businesses need to make sure that their supply chains are in a healthy and viable state.

Liquidation

This process will dissolve the organization's supply chain. In this strategy a company is closing and there will be no production of materials anymore. This strategy needs to be planned for to protect the relationships that have been developed in the supply chain.

WHAT KIND OF A CUSTOMER ARE YOU?

How easy is your company to deal with? Does your company pay their bills in a timely manner? I heard of one company where the first invoice that came in was thrown away. When the second invoice came in, it was thrown away too. If the company that was invoicing was persistent and sent a third invoice, it was then processed for payment. A practice like this hurts the supplier and does not create an attitude of cooperation.

How frequently do you change your order quantity? In many instances, it is not known until first thing in the morning what has to be shipped that day. This works fine if you are dealing with a relatively stable order that might vary 10 percent from day to day. In a fully operational mass production system, this should be the case. If the demand is going to vary more than 10 percent the supplier should be notified as soon as possible so the order can be made and shipped on time.

One of the critical factors for customers is to communicate specific needs. We must identify all of these needs whether they are specified or not to make sure they are satisfied with products or services. Many companies try to use salespeople as the mechanism for identifying customer needs. This is really not a reliable method as critical tolerances can be missed or critical characteristics may not be identified.

An example of how to share customer needs is to develop a cross-company team that is product line–specific and work with all the details. I have seen this in the automobile industry where critical characteristics, final use, delivery, and cost are discussed. As this team functions, all the issues are dug up and discussed so that problems can be found and resolved before a major crisis develops. This is where the concept of quality function deployment (QFD) can be used. The explanation of QFD can be found in many different books on quality concepts.

The ISO 9001:2000 standard has a clause that requires that customer requirements be identified. This is not just using the customer's purchase order to meet these requirements. In a very few cases using the customer's purchase order might work but in the majority of cases it will cause more problems later on as assumptions have to be made up front.

As the customer, the idea that has been promoted and supported in many industries is that I am always right and I can get exactly what I want. This is true as long as you do not take it to an extreme. Let me give you a few examples of what I consider a little extreme:

- Passing all inventory control functions and costs to your supplier and trying to hold the pricing the same.

- Sending out quality concerns for one small part, that could have been damaged at your location, and expecting root cause analysis to be completed within 14 days and returned.

- Trying to pass costs incurred by your business to your supplier.

As a customer, have you ever had an experience that made you say *wow!* These types of experiences are few and far between in the everyday business world. As a supplier your goal should be to have your customers feel this way. For many years, the Michigan Quality Council had a program that was called the "Quality Hero." This was a way of recognizing those who gave outstanding customer service. Each nomination that was approved received a certificate of recognition, a few novelties from the Quality Council, and a write-up in the local newspapers. It is a great deal easier to find a story about very disappointing service than it is to experience exceptional service. This program was a way to make the public aware of outstanding service.

One of the difficult areas today is for those businesses with direct people contact as customers, that is, hotels, airlines, retail, and so on. The mood of the customer can change and this can create difficult situations as their needs are attempted to be met. The consumers see themselves as customers but can often be very demanding and rude to the service agents, who can not do very much to change the situation. The main consideration in a situation like this is to be honest and do what you can as a service agent or get the help of your supervisor.

Let me share an example of an experience that my wife and I had with Amtrak. In 2002, we decided that taking Amtrak to Denver to the Annual ASQ Quality Congress would be a neat experience. It turned out to be a disaster because not one of the service agents told us the truth about what was going on. Upon arriving home we discovered that the customer service people had been telling us what they thought we wanted to hear and by this point it was too late for us to get any resolution to our difficulties through normal channels. It took the intervention of a senator from Michigan to finally get a refund.

All of these different areas show what kind of customer you are and determine if others will even want to do business with you.

INTEGRATING PROCESSES USING AGGREGATE PLANNING

A simple definition that I have heard for aggregate planning is two- to 12-month capacity planning. There are three components of this type of planning. The first is the business plan, which determines the strategy for capacity and production. The second is the production plan, which creates the production capacity utilization. The third is the master schedule, which establishes the production schedule for the specific products.

Ideally, the demand for a product will equal the capacity available. This is not the normal case, so production capacity needs to be adjusted to reflect the real demand. This process can be very easily distorted and complicated by very optimistic forecasts of product demand. Real demand data needs to be available wherever possible so that production capacity can be effectively used.

There are many factors that need to be considered on both the capacity and the demand side of the process. From the demand side, backorders, pricing, and special sales need to be considered with their impact on capacity. From the capacity side, hiring part-time workers, overtime for existing employees, hiring new workers need to be considered with their impact on the capacity. All of these areas are part of the effective management of the supply chain.

One of the basic problems that exists in business today is the issue of uneven demand. As a result of this, processes need to be put in place that will minimize the costs involved in leveling the demand and effectively using the available capacity. This is the goal of aggregate planning. In the area of operations management, you will find models and simulations that can be run to help optimize this process.

CONCLUSION

We have looked at many areas of management and developed organizational mission and vision statements that included supply chain behavior in them. The mission and vision statements are the overarching umbrella for the management of the business and should include the supply chain.

Forecasting is a very important tool to help increase the accuracy of the demand that will drive the production schedule. Several models were mentioned and can be researched in a good forecasting book for the details. The best model for a situation is the one that will give the least error.

Risk is an area that can be easily overlooked by customer and supplier because they assume that the other party has it covered. This inevitably causes problems in the future. Risks need to be defined and mitigated to the required levels for each organization. By doing this, many surprises and problems can be eliminated and both organizations benefit.

There are many different ways to develop competitive advantage and a strategy needs to be developed that will fit into your organization and operations.

Considering how you are viewed as a customer can help you remain in business. Companies are not only rationalizing (consolidating or removing) suppliers today, they are also rationalizing (choosing not to do business with) customers that do not perform well. This is a concept that has not been considered important because traditionally customers have felt that they were the driving force and could get whatever they wanted when they wanted it. This worked fine in an oversupply environment where every customer was crucial. In today's market, I have seen customers turned away because they demanded lower prices.

Aggregate planning is a process that involves the balancing of demand and capacity.

Supply chain management fits into the strategy of the entire business and the way that it operates.

KEYWORDS

Mission

Vision

Forecasting

Demand

Capacity

Risk

Aggregate planning

DISCUSSION QUESTIONS

1. How do the analysis factors described fit into the mission and vision statement of your company?

2. What is the best forecasting model to use in an organization?

3. Discuss some risks that might need to be considered in the management of the supply chain.

4. Evaluate your organization as to what type of customer they are.

5. Where is your company on the supply chain management maturity model? Why are they at this level?

6. What strategies are available to organizations for developing competitive advantage?

7. How does supply chain management fit into your company's organizational strategy?

4

Make or Buy: The First Step in Supply Chain Management

Deciding whether to make or buy a new product or service is the first decision that must be made in managing the supply chain. It determines where and how the supply chain will be managed. This decision impacts who the suppliers will be and determines what type of relationships will be required. Criteria for each decision can be identified and then it can be determined if they apply to a specific situation. The risks of each decision can be looked at with another set of criteria to evaluate the impact on each situation.

When a new product or service comes from the research and development area and the decision of whether to make the new product or buy it needs to made, in some cases it will be an obvious decision. But in many cases it is not as straightforward as we would like it to be. Some complications come into play when we consider subassemblies and partial products.

CAPACITY DECISIONS

Some questions that need to be considered regarding capacity are:

- Is the needed capacity available within the organization?
- What are the capital requirements to get the required capacity?
- Is the market for the product growing or shrinking?
- Can new capacity be added to the current process?

The above questions begin to set the framework for what needs to be discussed openly about the processes. In the previous chapter there was a discussion of aggregate planning and how capacity fits into the planning for production. A good understanding of your production capabilities and those of your supplier are required as capacity decisions are made.

MAKE DECISION DRIVERS

The Quantities Are Too Small

Sometimes the quantities needed are so small that it is not economical for a supplier to manufacture them or the cost to do it would be extremely high and would not be affordable for the new product. This can be very important to the initial introduction of the product. Both you and the supplier have to make money so the price of the product needs to reflect the costs required to produce it. It is very easy to get caught up in the grandiose ideas of a new product, not watch the costs, and end up in trouble. Perhaps existing equipment can be modified to get the small quantities and not require a significant capital investment. A very realistic projection of the demand for the new product has to be developed so that a cost estimate can be made to reflect the market potential for the new product.

No Supplier Is Interested in Providing This Need

There may be a hazard involved in the manufacture of the product and a supplier may not want to become involved with these requirements. It could involve getting new permits for handling and disposing of materials, which can take a considerable amount of time and money, or it may require some special material or equipment for processing. As rules and regulations change, the availability of capacity can change. Some companies may decide that the risks are not acceptable. There are many new requirements being placed on manufacturers today. RoHS and REACH are just a couple of the recent ones. RoHS is seeking to remove all of the heavy metals and hazardous materials from some electronics manufacturing processes. This seems easy to say but it is very difficult in many cases to maintain the capability of the products without currently listed hazardous materials being used in the process. REACH is a new requirement that all hazardous chemicals coming into the European Union be registered. This is a process that is still being defined and the fees are still being developed. This would make it the responsibility of the importer to have all of the proper registrations filed before material could come into the country. This could very easily become like a tariff on materials entering that area of the world.

Suppliers Can't Meet Exact Quality Specifications

Especially in the new product area, the requirements may easily exceed the capabilities of the supplier. If another decimal point is required in the tolerances, the supplier's equipment may not be capable of consistently meeting the tighter tolerances. This could be a result of gauge capabilities or it could be due to machine capabilities. You need a complete understanding of the product in order to determine the real requirements. Requirements need to be set as loosely as possible while maintaining product quality. This will increase the number of suppliers available for you to pick from.

When developing new products in the laboratory the tendency is to use the highest purity of materials available and then develop the process to make the product. When it is time to scale up to plant size, no consideration has been given to the impact of using a less pure material on yield and price. This can lead to very tight supplies of raw materials and maybe even no supply.

Control of Supply

As a company, you desire to maintain control of the supply and also maintain control of the price of the product. This is also a way of maintaining the business so it does not get treated like a commodity, causing the price to be driven down. The prices of commodity products fluctuate in the market and companies bid on them on a regular basis to see who is willing to cut their price to get the business. If the supply of the product is controlled, the price can be maintained where it is needed to make a profit and meet the market needs. A product can easily become a commodity when there is overcapacity in the market for the material.

Most profit is made when you are the first company to bring a product to the marketplace. As copycats develop, the product can become a commodity where companies are bidding against each other for the business.

Maintain Secret Processes and Products

Confidentiality is the issue here, and maintaining the competitive advantage that you have invested in. This is especially true for new products when they first come out in the market. Many new products and processes are not patented to maintain the confidentiality of the product or process. A patent does not give you exclusive access to the business. A patent can work like a disclosure, and then a competitor can develop ways to make the product better and not infringe on your patent. This can take a cut of your potential business. Many companies have a group that is designed to take apart the products of the competition and see what they can learn and how it can be applied to their products. This becomes harder if the products are made internally and the ingredients and processes are unknown outside the company.

Use Idle Equipment

If equipment exists and it is not running at full capacity, the incremental costs to run it may be significantly less than to pay another company to accomplish the task. As products change and processes are modified, equipment is not working at its full capacity, and this time and equipment can become available for some other use. This works very well in batch-type operations.

BUY DECISION DRIVERS

A Decision to Make Is Difficult to Reverse

Most decisions to make involve a capital investment, and it is difficult to reverse a decision where a significant sum of money has been spent and many individuals have agreed that this was the best way to proceed. A business leader does not want to admit that a mistake was made or something where his credibility might be challenged. Would the leader of your organization be willing to make a change that involved a major capital equipment write-off? Think about the response of the shareholders.

Maintaining Current Technology for a Non-Core Activity

The supplier may have state-of-the-art technology. If this is within his core competencies, the cutting-edge technology will be maintained while in your non-core environment it will lag behind. I am reminded of the company that stated in their history that their goal was to be the largest polystyrene producer in the world. As this company grew by acquisition some other product lines were obtained. If you wanted one of the other product lines and were preparing to reduce your supply base, would this be a wise decision?

Brand Awareness

A well-known brand in the eyes of the consumer can add credibility to the new product that you are trying to sell. One of the best examples of this is the brand name associated with gelatin. Have you heard of Jell-O? When you have someone looking for gelatin they will say they are looking for Jell-O. This has helped Jell-O market other products because of brand awareness.

More Flexibility

If you purchase material you have the flexibility to stop buying it at any time and the consequences can be a lot fewer than if a special facility or equipment had been purchased to do it. A contract can be negotiated for the benefit of both companies. Minor adjustments can be more easily handled with this method and good cooperation between companies can be maintained.

Less Overhead Required

The support staff to handle this additional business would not be needed and support would be handled by the vendor.

Difficult to Determine True Costs of the Make Decision

If the costs of the process and product are unclear, it may be best to look for a supplier. If new facilities are required and demand is unsure, then the costs would be unsure as well.

Now let's look at some of the risks that are involved in this decision.

Supplier Risks

With a new product, the supplier trusts that the business will grow and so will his profits. However, not every new product is successful. A company had modified some idle equipment to manufacture a new antioxidant that was to be an easy product to make. When they tried to make the product the only color they could get was red and they were looking for a water white product. The other problem was that the product produced was a gelatinous material rather than a liquid. This product did not last very long and the suppliers were disappointed in the results. In this case the large promised volumes never came to be.

Exit Barriers

If a new plant is built, it is very difficult to close the operation down. There are many liabilities that can be encountered when trying to close a business down. Today there are many governmental regulations that must be met when closing a plant down. One example is the cleanup that may be required if you try to shut down a plant that handled hazardous materials. When a plant is closed the remaining depreciation is written off and can be a large reduction in profits, requiring an explanation to Wall Street and the stockholders.

Difficult Economics

The economy where the product is being sold can change and the basis for the make decision may be challenged. When a major investment is made to install a new plant to supply current needs rather than to buy from existing suppliers, the selling price has to justify the decision. This type of situation can cost lots of money and cause tough decisions to be made.

Tied to Obsolete Technology

This can happen very easily if care is not taken. Technology is changing very rapidly and it is easy to fall behind and not really even be aware of it. Software is changing so fast that in some cases it is difficult to keep current with the capabilities that are available. When you go through a supply base reduction process and move multiple products to a new supplier, care needs to be taken in this area to make sure that you can stay up-to-date with the technology.

Long-Term Flexibility Could Be Lost

Depending on the decision and the arrangements that are made this could easily happen. Care needs to be taken in the way contracts are written and how and what changes can be made. Large capital investments may limit flexibility as well since they must recover their investments and perform as requested. Sometimes with special products the contracts get written with "take or pay" clauses in them and then the product must be used. When the supplier is required to make a special product that is purchased by only one customer, that customer must accept the material that they have told the supplier to make and will have to figure out how to use it.

Conversion Costs

These are incremental costs that are involved in making the product but in many cases are not fully understood or defined. This is an excellent measure to use when evaluating suppliers. This cost includes all the manufacturing costs to go from raw materials to the finished product in bulk. The conversion costs include things like labor, fuels, utilities, maintenance and repair, operating supplies, nonoperating supplies (workers compensation, insurance, taxes, and so on). With a good understanding of these costs for your own business you can do some very good estimating of your competitors' business.

Good Supplier Management Practices Are Required

Good supplier relationships are a must and there must be two-way communication. If there is not, the relationships fall apart and the blame game starts. When I describe the blame game I'm talking about the behavior of Jacques Nasser, President and CEO of Ford Motor Company, and John Lampe, Executive Vice President of Firestone, during the faulty tire issue in 2000 and 2001. If good supplier relationships existed, this type of behavior would not occur.

CONCLUSION

When you get involved in a make or buy decision, be careful not to jump to a quick decision but look at the reasons to go either way listed above and then consider the risks involved. If you do this you will end up with the best decision and your company should benefit from your choice. *Make* or *buy* decisions involve a lot of different considerations depending on the business or product and they must be considered very carefully to get the best results.

Get detailed with these decisions! Remember, a *make* decision can be very hard to reverse! If you have made the *buy* decision then you need to move to the supplier selection process and be just as careful and deliberate with that for the decision to be valuable to you and to your supplier.

KEYWORDS

Make

Buy

Risks

DISCUSSION QUESTIONS

1. How does the make or buy decision fit into supply chain management?

2. Name several reasons why a company would make a product.

3. Name several reasons why a company would buy a product.

4. What are some of the risks involved with a *make* decision?

5. What are some of the risks involved with a *buy* decision?

6. What are some things that need to be considered during the make or buy decision-making process?

5

Supplier Identification and Evaluation

How many suppliers does your company have? For an example, an automobile company can have as many as 50,000 suppliers. Think about the vastness of the task of managing all of these suppliers and getting the performance that your business requires. This is where a supply base reduction may be required to help get the supply base to a manageable level. There are many benefits to an effective supplier management system. Some of these are: better supplier performance on the critical characteristics for your operation, lower costs, lower inventories, less obsolete materials, quicker response to your customer needs, and good relationships with the suppliers.

In order to effectively reduce the raw material costs that a company incurs, the number of suppliers must be reduced to a manageable level. This chapter outlines a 15-step process that can be used to help with supply base reduction.

STEP 1: UPPER MANAGEMENT SUPPORT

One of the first things that the CEO needs to do is develop the structure for a steering committee of which he or she is the chair that receives regular progress reports and has regular meetings to receive updates on supply chain decisions that are being recommended and why. This committee can be a fairly large group of 10 to 20 people and still be functional as long as the leader is completely committed to the project. This is the group that will develop the mission and goals of the project and keep track of the progress toward the goals.

The mission of the project needs to be defined. An example of a mission is "We will reduce the number of suppliers to 100." Each one of the organizations that attempts a project like this needs to have the steering committee develop the mission statement. The mission statement needs to be communicated throughout the organization and everyone needs to understand the objective of the organization as the project moves ahead.

Upper management support is the critical starting point for a supply base reduction project. This project will take a significant amount of time and money to be done correctly. More than just lip service will be required to make it happen. The savings from a project like this are tremendous but the up-front costs can be significant and must be committed to so that the project can be completed.

The upper management group must all be for the project and support it wholeheartedly if it will be successful. There must also be some teeth in their commitment, and serious consequences for those who would try to hinder the process at any level. By "teeth" I mean disciplining people who do not help with the project or try to go counter to what the project is trying to accomplish.

When a project of this size is embarked on, some suppliers are going to lose business. This has to be known and understood by everyone involved. A strong commitment and support will be necessary as the business that was lost is attempted to be recovered. I will share a couple of examples of attempts to get lost business back.

In the first example, a company was in the running for one of the commodities that was being investigated. They were invited in to do a presentation, and one area where the company had trouble previously was the notification of material and process changes so that the customer could notify their customers of possible problems. Since this involved a chemical that was registered with the EPA it was required that the performance of the product be guaranteed and any changes that were made needed to be reported. When asked directly if they would notify the company of any material or process changes the answer was, "certify all of our plants and you will be fine." As a result, the supplier later found out that they had lost a large portion of business, and they even hired an ex-employee of the customer to try to get inside the customer's organization and get the business back.

In the second example, the supplier evaluation meeting was attended by just a couple of the supplier's sales representatives, who said they really did not want the business anyway. As a result the customer immediately moved the business to a new supplier. The supplier's CEO was not happy about the decision. He knew they could have received the business for all of North America as well as Europe and Asia for this customer. The CEOs of the two companies met on the golf course and the supplier tried to recover the lost business through friendship at the top level. As the two CEOs were playing golf, the CEO of the customer company told the CEO of the removed supplier that his company should have the business for this product line. This was an example where a customer had previously gone through a type of supply base reduction and never followed through, so the supplier did not believe that this customer would actually remove any business. If the customer CEO is not fully supporting the process, he undermines the entire process that is taking place, not even realizing that the process has just been destroyed by a casual comment to a friend. Other meeting places where this type of behavior may go on would be technical shows, conferences, and exhibits.

One way for you to convince upper management to support the reduction effort is to present a concrete example of savings to be realized. If an example is not available, the product group selected to work on first should be one that can show a high rate of return rapidly. Upper management talks money and as they see results they will be even more supportive of the process.

In most businesses today, raw material costs exceed labor and manufacturing costs by several times. Table 5.1 shows a small reduction in raw material costs.

The assumptions made in the table are: The raw material costs are 50 percent of sales and the overhead costs are 30 percent of sales. Labor costs are assumed to be 15 percent of sales. These percentages are a close reflection of typical ranges that occur in businesses today.

As can be seen from Table 5.1 a five percent reduction in the cost of raw materials yields a 50 percent improvement in profit performance. This type of impact is what upper management is looking for and it is a way to save lots of money. These types of changes should fall straight through to the bottom line of the organization.

Table 5.1   Small reduction in raw material costs.

	Case 1	Case 2
Sales dollars	$1,000,000	$1,000,000
Raw materials	$500,000	$475,000
Labor costs	$150,000	$150,000
Overhead costs	$300,000	$300,000
Total costs	$950,000	$925,000
Profit	$50,000	$75,000

Upper management must be convinced of the benefits and value of doing the project before it is started. Many times a simple table like the one shown above with figures from your own company can put some real numbers in front of them and show the potential savings for your business. This tends to bring the savings home.

Be sure not to let the project lag so that upper management has to ask what is happening with it. The project needs a success story and to get that requires that the project keep moving and getting some results. In the beginning when large amounts of time and money are being invested, upper management needs to know that progress is being made and that positive results are being seen.

STEP 2: PRODUCT GROUP SELECTION

How many materials do you buy and how many suppliers do you really have? This sounds like a simple question but it is amazing how many companies can not answer it easily. With companies growing by acquisition it is getting more and more common to see that the same material or part has several different numbers in the purchasing system because the companies were not effectively integrated during the acquisition. These types of problems will become evident when the process is being worked on and can save significant amounts of money when items can be consolidated into only one part and possibly only one supplier.

Data should be collected on all items purchased for several years and sorted by supplier. If you have multiple plant operations, the data will need to be consolidated by supplier. From here you will be able to see the large suppliers and what they are providing. This database also needs to be sorted by material so you can see who you are buying separate materials from; this will give you some indication of what types of materials can be shifted very easily. A review of the database to see if any of the products or materials are the same and can be consolidated should be done by the technical staff as well. If an approval process is in place for materials before they can be used, the approved suppliers for each location should be collected and sent to the steering committee as well. With all of this data, you can then develop product groups that match your type of business (that is, flavors, lubricants, oils, steels, fragrances, or dyes).

The starting point for upper management to tangibly show their support is to help you choose the product group that you will focus on. All materials that you purchase should be divided into groups based on similar characteristics. Examples would be solvents, salts, coatings, or ductwork.

Under the existing purchasing process these materials may be coming from a wide variety of different suppliers.

A report should be prepared showing the pounds or number purchased and dollars spent in each area by material and total. The annual purchases made in each group should be calculated. This shows where the largest purchases are. A Pareto analysis can be prepared on the annual purchases. The area that can produce the most return will be obvious from the Pareto analysis. This process will be discussed in Chapter 12.

The annual use figures need to be broken down by location in a multi-plant operation. All locations must be considered in the selection process. Long-range plans from upper management must be included in this step so that the chosen supplier is able to grow with the plan. New products and ventures that are planned need to be considered as the suppliers are chosen.

A report on the group selected should consist of volumes and dollars by supplier for each location for a multi-plant situation as well as totals by supplier. This document becomes the starting point for the analysis of the current process and where improvements can and need to be made.

In many organizations different products are sourced from different suppliers. If a company has gone through a number of mergers or acquisitions many more suppliers could be involved. When looking at a product group, the ability of a supplier to provide many of the products in the group should be considered. This type of information should be requested from the suppliers in their package. If a product approval process exists within the organization, this can be utilized if the need arises. If you happen to be in the chemical industry, one of the areas in which care will need to be taken is to expect chemical equivalents and not functional equivalents. Chemical equivalents should be almost direct replacements and a minimal amount of testing should be required for approval of a new supplier.

Functional equivalents are designed to perform the same function in a formula. Depending on the formula and the other components, a crashing-out effect (separation of an emulsion) or other separation could occur that destroys the use of the final product. An example would be in a shampoo where all the surfactants have risen to the top. The shampoo would not perform and the customer would be very dissatisfied with the product. When trying to get a functional equivalent approved, extensive testing may be required to make sure that the product remains stable with the new material.

Another area of concern should be product rationalization within your company. This is the situation where products are no longer to be manufactured. This often happens when a company has several products that really do the same function. An example of this would be when a company might make two or three different laundry detergents. A decision could be made to market only one of them. In order to make the operations more cost-effective and efficient, some of the products will be eliminated and the customers of these products will be switched to the remaining product. These types of discussions are made at higher levels in the sales and marketing departments. These decisions can change material requirements significantly and need to be put into the projections correctly so that volumes are representative of the material usage expected.

The goal of a process like this is not only to reduce the number of suppliers but also to build trusting relationships with suppliers and create a win–win situation for both organizations.

Traditionally, in the customer organization the ulterior motive was to try to drive costs down to the lowest possible level. One of the tactics that was used was to promise large orders to all suppliers. In some cases the same volumes were promised to two different groups of suppliers. What happened was the suppliers' expectations were raised as to what volume of business they could expect to receive and they quoted very good prices. But they were not given the expected (promised) volume of business. As a result of this behavior very poor relationships with little trust existed between these companies. The suppliers no longer trusted the customer organization and as time went on they did not even want their business. This shows the impact that dishonest practices can have on an organization and how the future of the organization can be changed as a result of this type of behavior. This can easily happen if the total focus is on getting the best price.

In another situation a supplier did not make one of the products a customer needed. The supplier had the capability and was willing to do it for the customer if they were willing to specify the amounts and buy what they said they would. This is a reasonable request and when complied with it worked out very well. The other part of this was that the supplier stopped making this product because of the process modifications that would have required them to upgrade their equipment and the decision was made to drop or rationalize this product line. By having a good relationship with this supplier the customer was told about the impending changes and was able to locate a new supplier before the material was completely gone and their process shut down.

STEP 3: TEAM MEMBER SELECTION

The supplier reduction team can be created directly by upper management or they can just appoint a chairperson and let that individual develop the team. An effective team is cross-functional with four to six members. The departments that need to be considered are:

- Quality

- Research and development

- Purchasing

- Technical support

- Operations

- Operators (floor workers)

Three departments are critical: quality, research and development, and purchasing. These three areas need to be represented because they have a large body of knowledge about the present system. Try to get people from those three departments who also have knowledge of other areas. The last three departments can add additional information about the suppliers that may not be readily known to the others. The operators can be critical as they are the ones that have contact with the material or are handling the incoming shipments. The input of the operators about how material comes in and how it works in the process can be very helpful in the reduction process.

Some training may need to be done as far as team dynamics and what is expected from the team. This is where upper management support is again critical. The team members must be willing to come to a consensus agreement as to what is best for the company and be willing to put some personal preferences behind if necessary. Employees can come from various backgrounds and experience levels and have developed preferences that could impact this process. Over the years, preference for one model or vendor can become ingrained in each employee.

Another area where upper management support will be needed is in requiring attendance at the meetings. A schedule of meetings needs to be developed by the team and every member of the team should be present to give their input on the decisions that are being made. Supervisors must not be allowed to hold team members for other assignments when the meetings are scheduled.

During the first meeting the team selects a person to run the meetings and lead the group. This needs to be done if the leader has not been appointed by upper management. The leader should be a person that can get things done and has a good rapport with all levels of the company. This process will be a powerful learning experience for everyone that is involved.

The meetings must be scheduled on a regular basis, which can be determined by the pace at which the project is expected to move, and everyone should be expected to attend. The meetings should be no more than two hours long and may be in different locations to spread some of the travel around. As a result of the planned duration for the meetings, promptness must be expected. Latecomers will have to be corrected or disciplined for the interruptions they are causing. The door to the meeting room may need to be locked at the start of the meeting to avoid interruptions by latecomers; normally a person will only be late once after top management sees in the minutes that they did not attend the meeting. The issue here is that the meetings must be important and consistent. Minutes of the meetings should be taken and sent to the steering committee so they know what is going on at all times. Goals and action items should be developed at each meeting and should be included in the minutes and used as a starting point for the next meeting.

If attendance becomes an issue, it will be up to the relevant manager or even top management to change the individual or manager to get the participation that is needed in the project. The attitude that needs to be transmitted is that it is a privilege to be a part of the project and it could be beneficial for them to do a good job on it.

The size of the team should only be four to six people so that coming to a consensus will not be a difficult issue and problems can be quickly resolved.

After a review of the report, the team that has been established needs to set a goal as to how many suppliers they feel might be able to handle the business. From this decision, the final number of needed suppliers can be developed.

STEP 4: CURRENT AND POSSIBLE SUPPLIERS LIST

From the analysis done in Step 2, the team makes a list of the current suppliers. All this tells them is who is supplying the products now. The product group needs to be analyzed as well to pick up all the approved suppliers. With the use of directories similar to Yellow Pages, other possible suppliers can be found. Some of the resources for finding other possible suppliers would be Thomas Register, regional buyers guides, purchasing directories, OPD directory, and the Internet. If these are not available on site, team members can be assigned to do research in a public library. The Web may be the method of choice in the technology age that we are in, but libraries continue to have very valuable information.

This stage of the process is similar to a brainstorming session where all of the current and possible suppliers are just being listed. No decisions or judgments are being made here. All that you are trying to accomplish is to make a list of companies that make the products that your company is working with. This is where the experience of the team members is important as they may know of other suppliers that can produce the materials that are being investigated.

Companies have processes for the approval of new vendors but that should be ignored at this point in the analysis. A good example of this is the production part approval process (PPAP) for the automobile industry. Other companies have different processes for getting materials on the approved lists. If a supplier is selected that is not on the list, the supplier will be required to go through the approval process and get the material on the approved list.

The output from this step will be a list of suppliers who can provide the group of products that are being investigated.

STEP 5: FIRST CUT

The first cut will reduce the number of suppliers identified in Step 4 to three. These suppliers will be the ones that receive further consideration. More suppliers can remain, but the remainder of the process will get cumbersome with many suppliers on the list. From this point on in the process you will be working with or considering only the three suppliers that remain after the first cut.

Each member of the team receives a list of all current and potential suppliers. The suppliers are removed one by one until only three remain by agreement of all the team members. (This process is very similar to lawyers removing qualified jurors to get to the correct number.) The gut feelings and experiences of the team members begin to come into play. This is where the team's knowledge of all the suppliers is shared and decisions are made.

All of the team members should participate in this and be able to give an explanation as to why they think that a supplier should be removed from the list. Listen to what is said and try to make sure the thinking is valid and that good reasons are being given. The team may be asked questions about this at the steering committee meetings when they are doing presentations of their progress. It would not be necessary to put all of this information into the minutes but it needs to be recorded somewhere so it is available for answering questions, if they arise.

When the first cut of the suppliers is made, the ones with the least or worst reputation with your organization are the ones that should be dropped first. That means that the final three should be the best perceived suppliers for your organization for this group of products.

STEP 6: NECESSARY ATTRIBUTES LIST

The list of attributes that the preferred (selected) supplier will have is developed by the team members. The attributes are specific to your company and the group of products being analyzed.

Normally there would be about 20 attributes defined so that a good picture of the supplier can be developed. The more defined the picture, the easier it will be to determine which supplier best fits the company. Attributes should cover areas like market share, long-range goals, global production where applicable, delivery ability, cooperative spirit, government regulations, computer systems, research and development, ability to change, quality system, and pricing scales. Additional attributes will be specific to your situation.

Some examples of attributes are:

1. What countries are you able to supply?

2. In what countries do you have manufacturing plants?

3. Can you guarantee supply to the locations in North America now?

4. Have efforts begun to form strategic alliances with raw material suppliers to ensure the availability of the needed materials?

5. Is demographic market research being done by market sector to identify current trends?

6. Can multiple product lines be supplied?

7. Will you keep us informed of process and material changes before they happen?

8. Are you open to joint R&D with secrecy agreements?

9. Are you willing to make custom products?

10. Are you willing to openly discuss costing information and documentation?

11. Are you willing to share cost savings that are a result of increased efficiency?

12. Are you able to adjust production to respond to current and upcoming regulations?

13. Is management support of alliances defined in writing?

14. Are you capable of making small to moderate batches of material?

15. Is your quality program certified?

16. Do you use SPC in your process and would these charts be available?

17. Can working teams be set up between companies with a point person at each company to be responsive within 24 hours?

18. Do you use distributors for your products to provide material to our locations?

19. Can distributor volume be included in overall volumes to calculate rates?

20. What is the business focus for growth over the next five years?

21. What type of technical service do you have?

22. Do you use just-in-time (JIT) in your process?

23. Are you involved in responsible care programs or other environmental programs?

24. Do you have electronic data interchange (EDI) capability and are you willing to use electronic transfer of funds?

25. Are you willing to register new products with the government as required?

Getting a good understanding of these areas of the supplier's business gives the team a good level playing field on which to make decisions. These attributes that are developed are the areas of the business that are critical to your business and must be met by the supplier in order to remain viable to your business.

The issue that is important here is how the supplier responds to these questions. This response will give the team an indication of what kind of relationship can be developed with this supplier.

These attributes will be evaluated at the meeting in the later steps.

STEP 7: MAJOR QUESTION PREPARATION

The team develops up to five serious questions that may encompass large parts of the attributes above. These questions should be difficult and allow the supplier to be creative in their solutions to the problems. As these questions are being developed, the team needs to think about what the answers to the questions will tell them about the supplier. The purpose of these questions is to help the team find the supplier that will best fit the company.

Examples of important questions would be: What type of quality program do you have in place now that will guarantee a quality product delivered to my company every time? Do you use SPC? Can you provide us with control charts for our products, if requested? Do you provide a certificate of analysis with each delivery?

These questions allow the supplier to tell you all about the quality system that they have in place throughout their organization. It will also give you an indication of their willingness to provide information to customers. If they do not do SPC, a follow-up question later could be to find out how they control their processes. This serves as a beginning question that will set the stage for how the supplier deals with their customers.

The major questions can cover a combination of attribute questions. These questions can be very specific, for example, plant locations are given and the supplier is asked how they would deliver to all of the different locations within 24 hours after receipt of an order from the customer. This delivery may not be practically possible, but how far out of the box is the supplier willing to think to meet the need presented? A question like this will give a very good indication of how willing the supplier is going to be to work with your organization. I have used this type of question to see how creative the company will be. Some of the responses that I have seen included offers for supplier-managed inventories in remote locations, designated stock set up at the supplier, and a special delivery system developed for a specific location to guarantee product availability. This is a chance for a supplier to really separate themselves from the competition by the way they are willing to think through these major questions and answer them. The team needs to thoughtfully develop these five questions so that the important issues to the customer are included in the questions. As a result, the responses to these questions will provide a great deal of information when the interviews are held with the supplier.

STEP 8: SUPPLIER PACKAGE PREPARATION

The team must identify the person at each supplier who has the authority to make decisions regarding future business commitments so the package can be sent to the correct person. If the package gets to the wrong person a lot of follow-up is required and many times very poor results are obtained. Suppliers have been embarrassed by the wrong person getting information and taking no action. Many times the person to whom this package should be sent is the president or a vice president, not a local sales representative. Many times the local sales representative would like to think that he or she has the power to negotiate with the organization but they usually do not have the authority to make the kind of decisions that would be required at this type of meeting. Their presence at the meeting is important as they need to know what is going on and it will set the tone of how they will be dealing with the customer in the future. Often this person can be located with a phone call by the committee chair or if necessary someone from the steering committee can obtain the contact information.

If the package gets sent to a local salesperson and he or she tries to fill out the information, incomplete or inaccurate information may be supplied because the salesperson may have limited access to the necessary information. This will become evident in the interview, and the potential to lose a significant portion of business is great. I have also seen the package be ignored by the salesperson and when the executive is contacted the salesperson is reprimanded for not acting on the request.

A package is prepared for each of the three suppliers. This package should include the list of attributes, the major questions, a summary of all materials in the product group with annual purchases (no current supplier listed), and a request for detailed information about the supplier's organization. The detailed information should include things like plant locations, plant sizes, ending dates of union contracts, financial statements that indicate the financial health of the organization, and a list of the company officers.

The supplier should understand that the attributes are what are to be discussed at the meeting and responses should be submitted on the major questions. Information about the company should also include organization charts, manufacturing locations, warehouses, and any other pertinent information for the type of material. A cost estimate for all of the materials should also be requested. The meeting date and time for the interview and discussion of the results from the completion of the information in the package should be included in the cover letter that is included in the package.

The importance of attendance at this meeting needs to be stressed. The attendees that are required may have to be specified. These should definitely include at least one vice president if not more. Both the sales and marketing department and the operations department also need to be represented at the meeting. This helps ensure that any questions can be answered by people from the correct areas.

STEP 9: INFORMATION PROVIDED TO SUPPLIERS

Step 8's package should be sent four to six weeks before the scheduled meeting date to make sure the needed people can be made available to attend. A letter from the team leader is included in the package that explains the process that the company is going through. The letter also gives the date and time of the supplier's presentation meeting, length and style of meeting (See Step 13), the location, and what needs to be returned and when. The package from Step 8 should also be faxed to the individual identified just before it is mailed to make sure a copy is received. The letter should help the supplier understand the importance of the meeting: to get business or to lose business. Many companies over the years have performed operations like this and then nothing changed, so the importance of attendance has been lost. These meetings will be making changes to operations and suppliers, and business will be shifted. Suppliers need to be aware that this will happen and that they need to be present or risk losing business.

In one case I was involved in the supplier said that they did not believe that any business would be moved because they thought that their products were so special that they could not be purchased from anyone else. When the switch was made a week later, that company lost $5 million in business. They were very surprised when they learned that their products were not that special and that the company was serious about the performance that was expected from suppliers.

In another case, I received a call from a selected supplier and was asked why they were being considered because they had been mistreated by a plant before and had been removed from the approved list. Someone else's product had been analyzed and they were accused of sending in the wrong material. An individual had created the problem who had no authority to remove anyone from the approved supplier list. The team had to deal with this and work through the past history and help the company get back on the approved list if they were selected. This was a difficult issue since it was in an organization that had grown by acquisition and had not been combined very well.

I have seen the president and vice president of a supplier organization ready to go on vacation at the time of the scheduled meeting. It was explained to them that if this business was important to them, they would be at this meeting. In this case both of these men showed up and received a significant portion of business. They were very pleased with the results and returned to their vacations a day later. As a customer you must be serious about how you are going to run your supplier process and communicate this to all of the suppliers and then do it. Consistency is important at this stage so that every supplier gets the same opportunity. Believe it or not, the suppliers themselves will determine which one is the best for your organization and the choice will become evident without having to let emotions get involved.

STEP 10: RANK AND WEIGHT ATTRIBUTE QUESTIONS

The team needs to rank the attribute questions. The whole team needs to decide the weight of importance for all of the attributes, from 1 to 3, with 3 being the most important. The team selects the top five attributes. Remember that not every attribute deserves to be ranked a 3. This is where through discussion the group will need to arrive at some consensus about the importance of each attribute. The discussion needs to center on how critical meeting each attribute is to the customer's business direction. It may take several meetings to come to an agreement on the ranking of the attribute questions.

This weighting and ranking will be used later. This is the beginning stage for the evaluation process that will go on after the meetings with suppliers. The team has to establish a level evaluation based on what is really important. The business plans and the future directions of your company will determine how important each one of the attributes will be. For example, if you are planning to do everything electronically and install a supply chain management software system that will automatically place orders to the supplier, then the electronic data interchange capabilities will be very important and rank a 3. Depending on the product or service, some of the attributes would be merely nice to have and these would be ranked 1 to see if the supplier can help in these areas.

At the conclusion of the discussion a form can be developed that will be used in the interview process that has the number of the attribute questions and the rankings (value) on it. An example is shown as Figure 5.1. The figure shows an example where only 18 attributes have been identified. This form will be used at the interview by the attendees from the customer's organization.

Date _____

Vendor _____

Question	1–5	Value	Total
1		3	
2		2	
3		3	
4		2	
5		1	
6		2	
7		3	
8		3	
9		1	
10		3	
11		2	
12		3	
13		1	
14		3	
15		2	
16		2	
17		3	
18		1	

Total _____

Is audit of their facilities necessary?   Y   N

Total/184 * 100 = Score _____

Figure 5.1   Interview question ranking form.

STEP 11: ATTRIBUTE GROUPING

The team will group the attributes together into specific areas such as production, quality, price, and so on. During the evaluation step these groupings will help show the team the supplier's weak areas. The attributes should be divided among the team members. Each member has a few for which they are responsible to see that the supplier deals with either in their presentation or through questions. All of the attributes must be dealt with during the presentation and dividing them up makes sure that all the team members are involved and different people are asking questions. This creates a high-level summary of the information obtained at the meeting that can be used to help evaluate the supplier after the meeting. The evaluation of this information can be given to suppliers who are not selected, to help them if they request it.

A form can be developed to tabulate the data in each of the areas that have been selected. The form might look like Figure 5.2. The attribute question numbers and the percentage ranking that would be developed in Step 14 for each of the questions are placed in the proper areas and averaged to

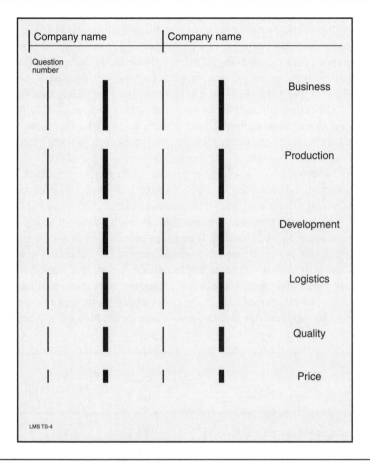

Figure 5.2 Form to tabulate the data in each of the areas that have been selected.

get the final numbers for each supplier. This form allows two companies to be compared on the same form.

STEP 12: DO YOUR HOMEWORK

Designated persons from the team should go to the local business library or use the Internet and learn all that is available about the suppliers that will be coming in. An annual report or a company history can be of great help. Copies of this information should be distributed to the team members and discussed at a meeting scheduled for shortly before the presentations.

These discussions should consider everything that has been learned and some areas that will be questioned at the meeting. Examples of this include the company focus, expansion plans, or environmental liabilities. Remember, you are looking for the best supplier for your company and you want to make sure that you have a good healthy supplier. One thing that you will need to see is that this supplier is open and honest with you and willing to work with your organization to help achieve your goals. The more that is learned at this stage, the better prepared for the meeting you will be and the better questions you will be able to ask.

As a company begins a supplier selection process, some research needs to be completed on potential suppliers. A good place to begin is in the local public library. There are many resources available to learn more about a supplier before and after they are selected. A few hours spent doing a little research (see Figures 5.3 and 5.4) can save millions of dollars wasted by the mistake of not really understanding the supplier. The data collected needs to be used like a resumé for the evaluation of the supplier. While building a relationship, a company needs to really evaluate and do some homework before jumping in. A study is needed to look at the business focus of the supplier. Are its core businesses focused toward the products

---

Ward's Business Directory of U.S. Private and Public Companies

Million Dollar Directory

International Directory of Company Histories

American Manufacturers Directory

Hoover's Handbook of American Business (Profiles 500 major U.S. companies)

Standard & Poors Corporation Records

Standard & Poors Register

Michigan Manufacturing Directory (This can be obtained for each specific state)

Job Seekers Guide to Private and Public Companies

Michigan Industrial Directory (This can be obtained for each specific state)

Moody's Industrial

Thomas Register

Directory of Corporate Affiliations (Three volumes)

Annual reports

Figure 5.3 Library resources.

Annual sales	Address	Phone
Officers	History	Current activity
Parent company	Accounting firm	Bank
Locations	Number of employees	Year founded
Credit rating	Public/private corporation	Trends in corporation
Assets		Liabilities
Fiscal year ends	Earnings	Legal firm
SIC codes	Import/export	Company history
Business type	Board of directors	Fax number
Telex	Sales	Square footage
Stock exchange traded on	Computers used	Major projects/ services
	Ticker symbol	
Benefits of employment	Human resource contact	Application procedure
		Stockholders
Long-term debt	Short-term debt	Capitalization
Stock data	Earnings and finance	
Credit rating	Key competitors	

Figure 5.4 Information from library resources.

that are needed? Sometimes this does not seem obvious, but as plants and businesses are sold, things can go along as attachments. A company does not want to be dependent on an attachment if it can be avoided. These issues need to be discussed openly with the supplier at the meeting or on a questionnaire sent to them.

Technical publications (examples for the chemical industry are shown in Figure 5.5) should be available and read by employees within the company who have an impact on business decisions so they know what is going on in the marketplace. As they read they need to be looking for their supplier, his competitors, and other products they use. In the *Chemical Market Reporter,* the "chemical profile" gives specific information about a chemical. The information includes a producer, which includes a supplier, plant location, and capacity. Other areas discussed are: demand, growth, price, uses, strength, weakness, and outlook. All of this information can be very useful as a company evaluates a material and supplier.

There are many ways to evaluate suppliers to get the best fit for your organization. The first thing that needs to be developed is a set of supplier criteria for the materials being purchased. By thinking these criteria

Chemical Market Reporter

Chemical Week

Chemical and Engineering News

Chemical Engineering Progress

Soap, Cosmetics, and Chemical Specialties

Happi

Paints and Coatings Industry

Adhesive Age

Chemical Processing

Chemical Engineering

Adhesives and Sealants Industry

American Laboratory

European Rubber Journal

Industrial Paint and Powder

Pollution Engineering

Research and Development

Modern Plastics

Powder Coating

Control

Processing

Plastics World

Rubber World

Urethanes Technology

Today's Chemist

Technology Business

Modern Paint and Coatings

Paper, Film, and Foil Converter

Power/Bulk Solids

Water and Waste Digest

Chemical Equipment

New Equipment Digest

Laboratory Equipment

Food and Drug Packaging

Industrial Product Bulletin

Plastic News

Packaging Digest

Rubber and Plastics News

Biomedical Products

Packaging World

Automotive News

Injection Molding

Manufacturing Engineering

Industry Week

Medical Plastics and Biomaterials

Plastics Technology

Scientific Computing and Automation

Medical Product Manufacturing News

Transport Topics

Food Technology

Quality Progress

Quality Digest

Industrial Hygiene

Pumps and Systems

Ultrapure Water

Chemical Management Review

Managing Automation

Genetic Engineering News

Control Solutions

Supply Chain Technology News

Pumps and Processes

Upside

Fast Company

Drug Discovery and Development

Quality

Modern Applications News

Figure 5.5   Technical publications for the chemical industry.

through, it will be evident what is important to consider when buying the materials. What factors in the purchasing of this material are really important to the company? This might mean that a company may not have to use only the larger producers if smaller ones can better meet the requirements. The selection process works best if it is customized for a group of materials and specifically for one company. Not all companies have the same requirements and needs, and so the supplier may be unique. Once the criteria have been developed, they can be sent to the supplier to provide a written reply, or the supplier can make a presentation where the criteria are discussed and many avenues of synergy are pursued. A numerical evaluation system should be set up to take some of the emotional impressions out of the evaluations.

The percent of sales of the supplier that your business will provide should be investigated. This number can be obtained with information found from the library research. What should be identified is total sales dollars. Converting your requirements to dollars and then dividing this number by the total sales dollars and multiplying by 100 gives the percent of their sales dollars that would be due to your business volume. Remember to consider what will happen to a supplier if a customer's volume significantly changes. One of the goals is to make sure that he will remain that company's supplier. A rule may be to not exceed 30 percent of the supplier's total sales. This allows some stability due to other customers.

STEP 13: INTERVIEWS

The supplier knows from their package that they have been given 1½ to two hours for their presentation. They should bring with them the proper people to make their presentation effective. They also know that only half of the time should be taken by the formal presentation. The remaining time should be questions and discussions between the supplier and the team members.

During the presentation meeting the supplier will really be indicating in many different ways how willing they are to work with your company. Discussions about giving help with product registrations, sharing research and development efforts, lucrative pricing arrangements, and how they are planning to meet the needs of your business at all locations can lead to an understanding of how the supplier is willing to cooperate and work with your company.

A limited number of people outside the team can attend from your company, but care needs to be taken not to overwhelm the supplier. The tone of the meeting needs to remain friendly and open so all necessary avenues can be explored.

In the interviews with the suppliers, the subject of product rationalization needs to be discussed so issues such as those in the preceding examples can be avoided and dealt with in a positive, proactive manner. Good communications and relationships are required to make this happen.

Product rationalization occurs because SKUs (stock keeping units) are desirable to be eliminated. If a product is produced and sold in 55 gallon drums, one-gallon containers, one-quart containers, one-pint containers, and five-gallon pails, each one of these would be a separate SKU. Inventories must be maintained by SKU and then converted to dollars for the accounting value of the inventory. This alludes to another reason for product rationalization—the reduction of costs by reducing amounts of products in the inventory. Reducing the number of SKUs also makes the inventory management process easier to accomplish.

During the interview, the list of attributes and the major questions will be discussed. The responses of the supplier will be evaluated to see how they answered and how willing they are to work with your organization. The main purpose of the interview is to evaluate the supplier and see how the attributes can be met by that supplier.

STEP 14: EVALUATION OF INTERVIEWS

The team has developed an evaluation sheet from the rankings of the attributes (see Figure 5.1). Each team member (and visitor, if the team chooses) can rate the supplier's answers to each attribute from zero to five after the interview is completed.

One team member is responsible for the mathematical extensions on each form and calculating the ratings for all the suppliers. Calculations should be done based on each attribute for later analysis.

Using Figure 5.2, the attribute questions are assigned to the business factors that they address. For each question, the total points from all the interview ranking forms would be divided by the total possible points for that question times 100 to get their percentage score for that question. This would be repeated for all the other questions. Then an average percentage for each business factor can be obtained. These forms can be adjusted to meet the needs of a specific group of products or a specific organization.

Summary forms can be developed by picking the number off Figures 5.1 and 5.2 so that all three suppliers can be looked at on one page. (Figure 5.6 is an example.)

If a specific question seems to bring concerns to the team, a form can be created that will be specific to the questions of concern. See Figure 5.7.

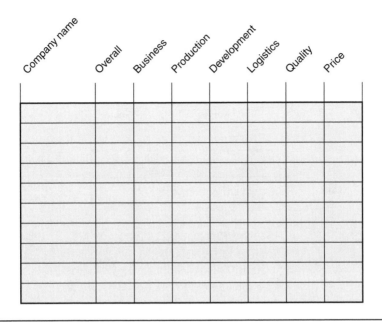

Figure 5.6   Example summary form to look at all three suppliers on one page.

Overall

Company name _____

Question number		Rating

Figure 5.7   Form specific to the questions of concern.

Vendor Summary

Vendor _____

Name	Score

Average score _____

Facilities audit

Y	N

Figure 5.8 A sample summary of the overall performance of the supplier organization.

A summary of the overall performance of the supplier organization can be compiled using all of the results from the organization. A summary form may look like Figure 5.8.

STEP 15: PREFERRED SUPPLIER SELECTION

By looking at the totals from the evaluation step the preferred supplier will be very obvious. If for some reason it is not, there is enough detail available at this point to do some extensive analysis and pick the best supplier. The mathematical data can be reviewed and correlated in many different ways to determine the best supplier.

By using mathematical analysis the emotional aspects are removed. I have seen the best supplier rise to the top in a variety of situations. Using the mathematical results helps to indicate an overall rating by the team members and the others. If necessary, more detail can be developed than in the charts shown previously but to this point I have not had to use further analysis to identify the best supplier for an organization.

The preferred supplier would be the one with the highest ranking. The strengths can be identified by looking at the business area breakdown. The overall rating will give the first evaluation point. Then look to the business areas for further breakdown. If specific questions are important these results can be looked at as well.

CONCLUSION

If these 15 steps are followed, your best supplier will be identified. As the implementation process of creating supplier alliances is begun, the benefits will be seen as dollars saved and an increase in the bottom line.

Now it's time to go on to the next product group and start with step one again. It will be easier this time, and you may find that those suppliers you have already chosen are the best suppliers for the next group as well. They already know your company and have indicated their desire to work with you.

KEYWORDS

Supply base reduction

Product rationalization

Supplier attributes

Interviews

Supplier selection

Supplier evaluation

DISCUSSION QUESTIONS

1. What are some considerations for determining a product group?

2. What type of information should be collected from the existing purchasing information database?

Continued

Continued

3. Who should receive the package of information at the supplier?

4. How do you determine who should be the correct person to receive the package?

5. What topics should be covered in the interview stage?

6. What are several attributes that a supplier should have?

7. Develop a major question for your organization.

8. How can product rationalization impact a supply base reduction process?

9. Why would a product be rationalized?

10. Why do executives need to be involved in a supply base reduction or modification process?

6

Selection of a Preferred Supplier

C ompanies today are looking for ways to reduce raw material costs. Some companies still believe that demanding reduced prices from suppliers is the way to control costs. A more effective way of controlling costs is by doing a supply base reduction process and a preferred supplier selection. When this process is completed successfully the best suppliers are found and real financial benefits as well as many intangible benefits can be obtained by both companies.

The impact of implementation of a preferred supplier program can be significant, as shown in Table 6.1. Implementing a preferred supplier program will directly increase the profit picture of the company.

The largest part of the cost of materials today is raw material costs. This is an area where large savings should be obtainable. Raw material costs in most businesses today are between 60 to 70 percent of sales. This is the area that will yield the largest savings the fastest, and these savings will drop through the process and show directly on the bottom line of financial

Table 6.1 The financial impact of implementation of a preferred supplier program.

Annual business volume (sales)	Raw materials % of sales	Percent annual savings	Annual savings $
$400 million	70%	2.0%	$5.6 million
		5.0%	$14.0 million
$10 million	70%	2.0%	$140,000
		5.0%	$350,000
$1 million	70%	2.0%	$14,000
		5.0%	$35,000

records. If money is not spent on raw materials and the same number of products are made, profit will increase. In simple accounting terms the top line revenue stays the same and cost of goods sold will decrease; as a result profit will increase.

Since upper management talks money, these kinds of potential savings will get their attention. Wall Street talks about company performance based on the profit of the company and dividends paid to shareholders. A change as dramatic as shown in Table 6.1 will get the analysts' attention as well.

Hopefully, at this point you are saying "How do I get the money?"

The real issue is taking potential savings and going through the process of implementation to move the potential savings to real savings.

CONTRACTS

Once a preferred supplier has been selected, it becomes the responsibility of the purchasing organization to put together a long-term (three to five years) contract for the supply of these materials as well as to manage the preferred supplier. The contract should contain some incentives to help speed the conversion of materials to the preferred supplier. As the contract is being developed, a relationship is being developed with the supplier's organization as well.

Many clauses can be added to contracts that are beneficial to both parties. Some examples are:

- The level of savings can be varied based on the volumes purchased.

- "Take or pay" clauses can guarantee the amount that will be purchased. These clauses will probably be involved if a special product is being made for your company.

- Given your best estimates for sales and production, estimate material usages and negotiate for a price based on that volume. Remember, the estimate should be the best you have and not inflated to try to get a better price from the supplier.

MANAGEMENT OF
PREFERRED SUPPLIER

A preferred supplier is best managed in a centralized manner. This becomes almost essential in a multi-plant situation to make sure that business goes to the preferred supplier. The corporate office sets up the system and local purchasing agents just issue the release against a blanket order. By setting up a system that functions like this, materials should not be able to be purchased from non-preferred suppliers, especially if the preferred supplier is approved. If this is not done, the full cooperation of all purchasing agents is a must. It may require some disciplinary warnings or actions to get people to change to the preferred supplier. Remember, implementing the preferred supplier is collecting the money and moving potential savings to real savings that can appear on the bottom line for your company.

Contracts with multiple locations and even multiple countries can be negotiated and monitored in this way. Better pricing and products can be obtained with larger volumes and adequate controls.

This can be a difficult area and may require some upper management intervention to convince some people that this work *must* be done. Importance must be given to this area of implementation. Research and development is always very busy and may put this on a back burner if it is not given priority by upper management. The longer the implementation takes, the less money you will be saving.

TRANSFERRING WORK TO PREFERRED SUPPLIER

Business should be moved to the selected preferred supplier as soon as possible. If the preferred supplier is an approved supplier, they should be given the material immediately.

Other similar products for which the preferred supplier is currently not approved should be investigated. The supplier should be asked if they have any chemical equivalent materials. If the preferred supplier has any, then samples should be requested and the necessary testing should begin. These tests should be completed as soon as possible so that the material can be purchased from the preferred supplier. In some situations a functional equivalent may need to be tested to try to increase the business from the preferred supplier as well as eliminate some of the non-preferred suppliers.

You should look at all the products that are purchased from the suppliers that have been eliminated. The idea behind implementation would be ideally not to buy anything from these vendors.

Three steps that need to be implemented for the new preferred supplier are:

1. If the preferred supplier is already approved as an alternate, the purchase should be immediately moved to the preferred supplier. If the preferred supplier is not approved, they must be contacted to see if they have a chemical equivalent product first. If they do,

get samples of the materials and test them as required by the system in your company.

2. The next step would be to discuss functional equivalents to replace the remaining products coming from eliminated suppliers. This may be more difficult since in many cases they may require a formula change and much more testing. These should be pursued if the volume of material purchased is warranted by the savings that could be obtained.

3. Thirdly, the discussion needs to be opened up as far as the preferred supplier making the offset material for you. This is where guaranteed volumes and so on may come into play. If you have a large volume it may well be worth the supplier's time to make it for you, if the equipment is available. If the supplier is currently not making the products for the marketplace for a variety of reasons, see if they would be willing to make them for your use only.

Beware of product rationalization within your organization! As products are eliminated from a product line, so are some raw materials. You need to be aware of any such plans from the marketing area so you don't end up making a lot of false promises and wasting your suppliers' time and resources as well as those of your organization.

Other possible synergies between the supplier and customer need to be investigated to try to reduce the costs for both businesses.

You need to get as much volume of business to the preferred supplier as possible as soon as possible so you can begin to reap the benefits of a preferred supplier.

TOLLING ARRANGEMENTS AND COST EFFECTS

Another area to consider in negotiations is tolling arrangements and cost effects on total contract. You need to communicate to all buyers that individual prices may vary but overall volume to the preferred supplier is what will really save the company money. In some cases individual buyers will not be given pricing information. The special pricing obtained from the preferred supplier *must not* be shopped on the market, especially to non-preferred suppliers. The non-preferred supplier may try to undercut the preferred supplier.

I saw a case where a supplier that had been eliminated came back and offered a material at $0.50 per pound less than it was being purchased for on the preferred contract. The first response was to talk to the preferred supplier and discuss this issue. It was learned that there was no way that the product could be produced for the price being offered. The preferred supplier commented that this could be a way of the eliminated supplier liquidating inventory. It was learned a few weeks later that the inventory was being eliminated and no more of this material was being made by that supplier. By working with the preferred supplier, a relationship was maintained and this organization did not fall into the trap that the eliminated supplier was trying to set. Businesses will try many different ways to get business, but with a preferred supplier we have made a commitment to that organization. We must work hard to maintain that commitment.

Communicate to all departments the need to work with the preferred suppliers and to develop ways to reduce costs for both companies.

BUILDING A POSITIVE RELATIONSHIP

Credibility in the marketplace can have a positive impact on whether customers and companies are willing to do business with your company. If you treat your suppliers well, word gets around, and others will be willing to work with you as new technology is developed. If you "beat up" your suppliers, that word gets around also, and other suppliers look elsewhere to build their business and share technology.

An example of this today can be found in the domestic automobile industry. Automakers continue to demand price reductions from their suppliers and increased performance at the same time. This has caused a number of them to go bankrupt, while others are working on changing the focus of their businesses.

The old adage "what goes around comes around" is very true in supplier relationships too. If you treat your supplier well they will return the favor. There can be no greed involved in an effective preferred supplier implementation. Cross-functional and cross-organizational teams should be created and should visit each other's facilities and learn about each other's businesses. This could be done by an outside auditor checking the quality process, but this keeps the relationship very impersonal. By visiting the site, a sense of the cooperative spirit is gained that can far outweigh any flaws in a quality system, which can be worked out together.

Once technical people from both companies begin to talk, problems can often be resolved rapidly and before any crisis occurs. This is also a way of learning about new technology that is in development. It may help your organization develop new products as well as improve existing ones. Being first to market with new products can be very beneficial for both organizations and this may open up the opportunity for some exclusivity agreements. This may involve your exclusive use of the product for a given number of years until the product is established in the market. Competitors will have to develop another source of the new material which will take time and give you a chance to get your new product established in the marketplace.

Have you ever worked for a company that did not have credibility in the marketplace and try to convince suppliers that you are serious "this time?" This is a very difficult situation to be in and sometimes some dramatic moves or changes must occur for you to really get the supplier's attention. When it is only your word, it may be a very hard sell. When trust has been broken it takes a long time to regain that trust. Good faith will have to be demonstrated on a small scale before trust will begin to be reestablished.

I was involved in a situation where consolidation of suppliers was being attempted for North America and Europe. One supplier had a particular capability already in place and many of their products were already approved for use. At first it seemed like the obvious answer was to use this supplier that seemed to meet the company's needs perfectly. As the consolidation process continued, to make sure that this was the best supplier a meeting was set up with the supplier to discuss how the companies could work together. This is where the surprise happened. The supplier's representatives told the customer that they did not want their business because of their past performance. This was an opportunity lost for both organizations because of a credibility issue that had developed over the years. The customer organization could not understand why this happened. I later learned that many commitments had been made over the years and never delivered on, and the supplier had decided that they were not going to deal with that type of organization anymore.

Have you ever seen companies put out lists of products to bid on and they bid the same product to several suppliers? This might get them a volume break, but it really can destroy credibility and the potential to build a preferred supplier relationship.

I saw an organization that tried this and it worked well for a little while. Then they ended up getting take or pay clauses in their contracts because of this behavior. Both parties should benefit from a good relationship.

BUILDING AWARENESS OF
THE RELATIONSHIP

A special plaque should be designed to give to the selected (preferred) supplier. Remember, this plaque will probably end up on the wall in the supplier's lobby so it should look as nice as possible.

A presentation should be set up where upper management from both companies present and receive the plaque. Pictures should be taken and published in both companies' newsletters, local newspapers, and trade journals. This helps to communicate to both organizations what is going on.

Those people from both companies that will be involved directly in the relationship should be given some type of give-aways from both companies as a way of reminding them what is going on and to get their support for it. The power of a portfolio or a pen to act as a reminder of the relationship that exists with the organization depicted on that pen or portfolio is amazing. This can be a few dollars well spent to gain the support of many people in both organizations.

This may be viewed by some top managers as time-consuming, wasting good money, and not beneficial, but the goodwill and support that this will show can help the organization build a better relationship with the supplier. This is a simple way to show the support of top management.

THE PURCHASING DEPARTMENT

A preferred supplier program changes the role of the purchasing department. The new responsibilities of the purchasing department include:

- Making sure technical exchanges are occurring. This may be accomplished by using a seminar format at each organization to share technology and ideas. (The technical group may set up and pick the topics of interest.)

- Organizing meetings between top management from both companies.

- Managing order placement to correct suppliers.

- Working with research and development to move more and more business to preferred suppliers.

- Checking pricing semiannually to be sure you are still in the correct area.

- Organizing meetings to discuss programs and areas to improve.

- Keeping suppliers informed of any major changes in demand.

- Supplying suppliers with projected requirements.

If a supplier has been removed before and the door has been opened again, the supplier needs to deliver samples, prices, or whatever else is promised in a very timely manner if credibility will be maintained and the possibility of being reinstated as a good supplier is to remain open.

Sample testing commitments need to be pushed to make sure they remain fresh in the chemist's mind and that the materials submitted will get a fair test.

During the process of implementation, purchasing must begin its new role, but it also really needs support from the technical areas as well as research and development to really begin to benefit from the preferred supplier.

A record should be kept of products moved and savings accrued. This record can be used to show upper management the benefits that they have received from the preferred supplier. This is important because top management talks in terms of money and the results need to be put in terms that will get their attention.

Tickle files must be set up to keep the priorities of the product moves on track so the greatest benefit can be obtained. It may help if savings can be estimated so that it can be used as an encourager to have the technical people move a little faster on these issues.

Purchasing departments will see some major changes as they begin to manage a small number of suppliers rather than chase lots of suppliers to get the lowest price. A different paradigm will take shape. The preferred supplier will be working with them to help make both businesses better. The biggest shift is that purchasing may not be in complete control of the situation anymore. For some departments this will be a difficult change to deal with.

DRIVING SUPPLIER PRODUCT IMPROVEMENT

What characteristic of the supplier's product can be changed and reduce costs without changing the quality of your finished product? This is a very difficult question for most businesses to answer because they do not understand their own processes that well. The answer requires a very detailed understanding of both operations and products. A team with members from both companies can begin to investigate this question and supply some problem-solving tools to help them get some ideas of where the most savings can be obtained.

One of the problem-solving tools that can be used is *brainstorming*. This is where possible solutions, regardless of how far out they may seem, are listed just to get thoughts started. After the list has been made, each one of the possibilities is discussed to see if it might really work. The ones that might really work then are investigated further to see if any are a possible solution. As the investigation begins, the application of other tools will need to be examined.

A way to put previous problems behind you is to try to deal with the situation openly and look at what really happened and then move on to what is being or has been done to prevent the situation from happening again.

A situation existed where a raw material supplier was causing a very bad color problem in a finished product. The supplier was disqualified but never given any information about the problem. After repeated attempts to find out what could be done to resolve the problem, the supplier just gave up. Needless to say, the supplier was not happy. The subject came up during a supply base reduction meeting. Very little information was documented so we started the requalification process, which turned out to be successful. The difficult part turned out to be getting the people that were involved initially to put the situation behind them. As it turned out, their product was better than what was needed so another supplier was given the business, but this one remained as a qualified alternate.

"Once burned—shame on you; twice burned—shame on me!" This is the attitude that is created when trust has been broken. It may be a long process to restore the trust back into a relationship. After a very difficult experience, it will be hard to get all of the business back again. Reestablishing the relationship and trust requires some business so that trust can begin to be developed again, and as measures are taken to prevent recurrence of the problem the possibility for more business may exist as the relationship strengthens.

If you had a supplier that delivered bad product and would not own up to the fact that it was bad or the supplier could not deliver material as needed or agreed to, would you buy from them again? Probably not, but would you be willing to work with that supplier to help them improve?

What would it take to get you to purchase material from that supplier again? This is where unrealistic expectations can develop but must not be allowed to influence the process. Mistakes can be made and processes can be improved. Are we willing to work with suppliers to help them improve?

MANAGING THE SUPPLIER RELATIONSHIP

What is involved in managing a supplier? The performance of the supplier needs to be tracked and ways to do things better need to be looked into. A cross-functional team with members from both companies needs to meet regularly and look at where they have been and where they are going. The purchasing department will become a clearinghouse for all of the information about the suppliers.

Quality and delivery problems should be able to be resolved very quickly to the benefit of both parties.

Regular monthly meetings should be set up with local sales representatives to discuss what is projected for the next month. The sales representatives should also meet with the technical groups to get updates on new product launches and possible requirements for other products. This is another way to communicate news back and forth between the organizations.

The purchasing department needs to track plant purchases and volumes to see if contracts are being abided by and volumes are being made as promised. If difficulties are observed, this needs to be discussed with the supplier early on in the process so that surprises are eliminated and the issues can be resolved. We need to treat the supplier like we would like to be treated.

I had a plant purchasing manager that had developed a friendship with the salesperson from one of the eliminated suppliers. He continued to try to give business to the removed supplier. It took top management involvement to get this issue resolved and the supplier removed. The supplier then hired a new salesperson from the customer company who tried to get the business back through the contacts that he had inside the company. It did not work. Companies will try all kinds of tactics to get business.

Invoices will need to be verified by the purchasing department to make sure discounted, agreed-upon prices are being applied.

If payment terms were written into the contract, the purchasing department needs to follow up with the accounting department to make sure that checks are being mailed in a timely manner as agreed upon.

A limited amount of time should be left for talking with other suppliers. When talking with other suppliers, purchasing needs to be aware of new technology or ideas and pass this information on to the technical group so they are able to follow up if they have an interest.

New technology from the preferred supplier should be used first, if possible. The real goal here is to keep your company on the cutting edge of technology, be able to launch new products quickly, and reap the benefits of being first in the market.

Playing catch-up and copying never make you a leading company. The real money is made by being first to market and leading the way.

People at all levels of the organization need to be involved. Think about a restaurant that you frequent. What am I there for? What are the cook, servers, hostess there for? If you go back many times and become acquaintances (friends) with these folks, what happens? If you treat them well, what happens? You find that these people recognize you and want to serve your needs. The same principle applies in the business world as well. If two companies can work together, both can benefit from each other.

CONCLUSION

Having many suppliers makes the supplier management process very difficult for the purchasing department. By reducing the number of suppliers and establishing relationships at various levels between the organizations, it becomes much easier for the purchasing department to manage. A good intercompany communication process needs to be set up so that everyone that works with a supplier knows what is going on. The benefits of having a great preferred supplier will show up on the bottom-line performance of the business.

KEYWORDS

Preferred supplier

Teams

Relationships

DISCUSSION QUESTIONS

1. What are some of the benefits of having a preferred supplier?

2. Is recognition of a preferred supplier important? Why?

3. Why do all departments from both companies need to work together?

4. What is the new role of purchasing when using preferred suppliers?

5. What should the role of research and development be in a preferred supplier relationship?

7

International Considerations

When working with suppliers in other parts of the world, especially Asia, differences in the culture must be considered in order to have an effective relationship.

As Americans, it is often assumed that everybody does things the way we do and that our way is the only right way. It is easy to develop this idea if you have never been exposed to another culture.

If you visit another country for a vacation, it is very easy to insulate yourself from the real culture and just sightsee, and do what you need to do while you are there and return to the security of your homeland. Assuming that everything should be done as in the United States, and making comments and acting like this, is what created the term "ugly American." This type of approach will not work in building relationships with suppliers on a global scale. To be successful, the culture must be understood and the relationship must grow in the context of the culture. Sometimes people need to be hired that understand and are able to work in both cultures to build a successful relationship.

LANGUAGE

The first big difference is the supplier's language. A relationship must be built in their language. Dealing in their language makes things so much easier to get done. Not expecting them to speak and read English shows that we respect and really care about them for who they are.

When my family was living in Manila we were told that we could get by using English and we didn't need to learn a Filipino language. After a few months in the country, we hired a language tutor to help us learn some of the language so we could begin to converse with the people in their language. This was exciting! It was like a wall of ice melted between us and the people, and they seemed more willing to deal with us at a deeper level.

FAMILY

A second difference is the concept of the family. The definition of the family in many countries extends far beyond the immediate family and even includes first and second cousins. There is a felt responsibility to care for all members of the family to the best of one's ability. An example of this would be a housekeeper in a city sending almost all of her salary home to help a relative with school.

Another part of the concept of family is the pressure it produces, and also that what is done to a member or what happens to a member is viewed as a reflection on the entire family. By disciplining an employee, rather than just trying to correct a problem and make a better employee, you are bringing shame to the family. In many cases the family may seek revenge. This can have a definite impact on the way that businesses are operated. Supervisors may not be willing to discharge an incompetent employee for fear of what the relatives of the discharged person might actually do, such as physical harm, reprimands for the harsh treatment, or threats.

The impact of the family can have an effect both on the availability and quality of the product produced. This must be considered in building relationships.

CRITICISM AND SHAME

A third difference is that Asians generally do not differentiate the person from the role that he is playing. Realizing this, if you criticize a person's work, it is taken very personally as a criticism of that person and it is a reflection of "shame" on his family. The concept of shame is a very important issue that Westerners need to be aware of in Eastern cultures. It is not a driver in our culture but it is a very strong driver in many other cultures and needs to be considered in our actions and decisions.

INTERPERSONAL RELATIONSHIPS

A fourth difference involves the concept of "smooth interpersonal relationships." This is a nonconfrontational attitude and the desire not to receive or give a negative response.

One of the three primary characteristics of smooth interpersonal relationships is stating an unpleasant truth or opinion in a manner that is calculated to please, or broaching a potentially unpleasant situation or subject in a manner that allows the person to retreat.

In the Asian context, rebuke is handled with tact. Great concern is shown for the person's family and their health and welfare. Personal matters may be discussed in detail first. Then the person that is being rebuked is told that they are still accepted and will be treated the same as before. Now the complaint is explained in as pleasant a way as possible and even may be padded with a little velvet to soften it.

This can look like a useless, time-wasting, indirect, and hypocritical way of handling situations. In the American context, we want efficiency and frankness. But we must remember that we are dealing on their turf and they are the ones that are really in control.

A second characteristic of smooth interpersonal relationships is the power that peers, groups, or family have in getting things that they want. Being accepted and doing what the group wants becomes more important than the one-on-one meeting that I have set up.

A third characteristic of smooth interpersonal relationships is the use of a go-between as a mediator to help resolve difficult situations. This person uses tact and can get problems resolved for both sides without confrontation. This is just the opposite of what North Americans do, which can really create some problems if we are not aware of it.

Another part of smooth interpersonal relationships is telling you what they think you want to hear and not wanting to say no.

Cigarettes are sold individually on the street corner successfully because if a person buys an entire pack of cigarettes, he is unable to say no if someone asks for one. As a result people buy them one at a time on the street corners to avoid the situation.

What does "yes" really mean? If an Asian agrees to meet with you, will he show up if he says yes? He may not, for four reasons:

1. If you have only met a few times there is not much of a relationship so his obligation may not be very high.

2. Maybe he had another commitment already and didn't want to hurt your feelings by saying no.

3. Maybe he would like to come but he is really not sure that you want him to come. Another persistent attempt needs to be made.

4. Maybe he meant that he will probably meet you more or less at that time, but he won't promise because something might come up.

If you want to have someone present you must be sincere and persistent (invite several times) in your invitation!

The other thing about meetings is that the higher your status, the later you should arrive for a meeting. As you can already see, the clock does not really run meetings like it does in the United States. To be effective we need to be sensitive to this and expect it. I have set meeting times here in the States and had latecomers arrive and have had to repeat a lot of information to get the late people up to speed. This can be very frustrating and time-wasting for the others in the meeting. I have gone to the extreme of locking the door when the meeting starts and taking attendance. The meeting agenda is covered and the minutes are distributed. The late people are shown as absent. This gets the boss's attention and it normally does not happen more than once. The other thing that I have seen done is to calculate the value of the time wasted by the latecomers not being present. This puts the problem in terms that management can and will understand. These techniques will work in the United States but they will not work in other cultures.

In the Asian culture there is a concept of debt that differs from the way we view it. How debt is repaid depends on the status of the lender. The highest form of debt is called a debt of gratitude and this can never be repaid. It is like the debt you owe your parents or for saving someone's life. These can also enter into the business world and affect how business decisions are made.

When you are meeting in a foreign country or with people from a foreign country there will probably be some sort of food there. You *must* eat some. It is part of the hospitality of their culture and they will be very offended if you refuse to eat. Even the Amish in the United States have very similar values. If you are working with the men and the ladies bring some dessert, it would be very improper for you to refuse to eat the dessert, as well as embarrassing to the Amish men. These kinds of actions can inhibit the growth of relationships that are required to effectively manage businesses and the supply chain.

In foreign countries, one way to get things done is with money. This will work for a while but you had better have real deep pockets if you hope to continue to rely on this. Bribes are acceptable in some cultures as a way to get things done and sometimes even expected. By building an effective relationship it can become easier to get the things that are needed without the bribes.

The better way to do business is with relationships. Relationships are very important in the Asian culture and must be considered if a good supplier relationship is to be developed and maintained. The relationship must be built on trust and respect for the individuals. You must be viewed as a friend and someone that cares about them as an individual. By building good relationships, tasks will be accomplished and the needs of your business will be met. The individuals that work in the government offices in the foreign countries have a job to do and that may not be to get things done your way. By understanding the system and working with the people that are your friends, the necessary jobs can be accomplished in a timely manner. If you try to push your way through their system you will run into some very serious roadblocks that will cost you unnecessary time and money. Again, remember the importance of relationships.

POVERTY

As you begin to deal with third-world developing countries, you will see lots of what appears to be poverty by United States standards. You must understand the context and see through the culture's values rather than apply United States standards. If a person is able to eat on one dollar a day that does not necessarily mean that they are poor. The news media here in the United States has done a good job of showing people living on the Smokey Mountain just outside Manila. Smokey Mountain is the garbage dump for the city and it really is a big compost pile. Just about everything that can be recycled is recycled. The people living on the dump are living there by choice to protect their scavenging rights so that another person does not move in and take over. These people are considered wealthy in their country. Many of them travel to the United States several times per year. The concept that needs to be understood is that we cannot judge poverty only by the way a person is living.

APPEARANCE AND BUYING HABITS

Another example of cultural differences would be that personal appearance is often more important than where one lives. As a result an executive secretary will wear the latest fashions and look like she really fits into the business world, but may live in a squatter shack. The concept of what is important is different and we need to understand this as we deal with foreign companies.

Things that Americans take for granted as essential purchases are not the same in Asia. An Asian will purchase a television before they will buy a refrigerator. They can go to the market every day and get what they need and use it so there is no need for a refrigerator. The other issue that many countries have is a source of reliable electricity. Even in the city of Manila power outages happened almost every day because of the lack of capacity. When the power went out you had no idea when it would come back on and no way to check on any progress. As a result, the society has learned to live in this environment and look ahead. Homes have elevated water tanks so that when the electricity is on the tank can be filled and there will be water in the house when the electricity is off. Adjustments have been made to live within the circumstances and the people do fine. As we try to do business there we need to remember that our business must be done on their terms and we can not change them or their country to get what we want.

Negotiations in an environment like this can be a real challenge when you request a price and you receive the answer "It's up to you." Getting an answer like this is a challenge because how you respond will determine whether you really care about these people. They have a price that they are expecting and want you to negotiate with them to get that price. Care needs to be taken that it does not appear that you are trying to take advantage of them or the deal could easily fall through. To get things off on the right foot you will need to learn about their families and share information about yours and other personal areas before the business can even begin. You may also have to visit some of the important sites of their city that they want to show you before the business can start. Remember that you are their guests, you will be treated as guests, and you need to be gracious for what they are willing to do for you. You can not set the schedule of how things are going to happen and how fast things will move; that is their responsibility and you have to comply.

GOVERNMENT

The governments in the Asian countries do not function as ours. In many of the countries only a few families control the wealth of the country. This type of situation can bring in many outside issues for supplier relationships, as well as surprises.

An example of this was the freezing of all exports of palm kernel oil from Indonesia by the president of the country. If I were being supplied palm kernel oil from Indonesia I would have had an immediate problem that no contract could solve.

Another example was when China threw out all multilevel marketing companies. At the time, a cleaning products company was investigating the possibility of building some new facilities in that country. They had to regroup and form other plans for doing business there.

In the Philippines a law was passed that made it illegal to import parts for the repair of fossil fuel electricity generation plants. The goal was to complete their nuclear power plant, which would supply electricity for the larger part of the nation. When Marcos lost the election, Cory Aquino immediately stopped the construction of the nuclear power plant because she felt it was too dangerous. The country was in a serious bind, with not enough electricity as a result of the fossil fuel power plants breaking down with no replacement parts on hand. This had an impact on foreign businesses and many considered leaving. These situations as well need to be considered when dealing with foreign countries.

As we read the newspapers and listen to the news these days, we hear a lot of stories about problems with the food industry in China. For various reasons they are allowed to use materials in that country that are not allowed in the United States. We have to be aware of this and run our businesses accordingly. If there is a question about a banned substance here we need to be prepared to deal with the situation. One concept that needs to be understood is that the world does not revolve around the United States. Our laws do not rule the world and we can not expect them to. We need to be able to work in foreign environments and work for the benefit of both countries.

In some Asian countries prices often are not set by what the market will bear but are completely controlled by the government and have no reflection on true costs. For example, the cost of the ride on a jeepney bus was controlled by the president of the Philippines, as well as the price of gasoline. Both prices could be changed at will by the president. These types of actions have caused strikes by the drivers that left many people stranded.

SUPPLIER CONSIDERATIONS

If you are working with a United States supplier that has an office or manufacturing facility in Asia there will be a different relationship on either side of the ocean. Even though it is a U.S. company, the principles of the Asian culture will be operating in Asia.

Today some companies are trying to become "global" by setting up distribution points in other parts of the world. As a manufacturer this may help my supply chain and get me uniform material around the world.

As nationalistic views continue to grow in the developing nations, more of them are requiring that manufacturing be done in their country rather than just allowing materials to be exported. To do this requires foreign investment that developing nations need and want so this trend will probably continue to grow.

China, New Zealand, and the Philippines all require manufacturing to be done in their countries. By doing this these governments are creating more jobs for their own people. In other countries companies are required to have a partner in order to establish a facility in the country.

You should take courses to help you learn some of the local language. You should at a minimum be able to greet the people in their own language to show them you respect them enough to be willing to try to learn their language.

Learning about the culture can be a little more difficult. Books from the State Department or even the library do not deal with cultural issues. They tend to be more touristy or cover governmental type issues. One source of cultural information is to contact a mission organization that has missionaries in the country in which you are interested. They should be able to give you some very good information about the culture of the country.

When my wife and I were running a guest house in Manila a few years ago we learned how to shelter visitors from the culture. Basically this was done by us dealing with the nationals for the visitor, and they typically didn't know or understand what was really happening. The food served at the guest house was semi-Western so it served as a buffer zone between the two cultures. If you want to get involved and understand the local culture, it is going to take some effort on your part. As the nationals see this they will be more than willing to help you learn and laugh with you at your mistakes.

Gestures used can be very important. These have different interpretations in different cultures. One major difference is signaling with palm up and moving fingers versus signaling with palm down and moving your fingers. Another is calling a person's name loudly in a crowd versus making a hissing noise. The North American way is considered rude and inconsiderate elsewhere.

Many Asian countries are located in the tropical area of the world. Due to the heat most people take a siesta for an hour to an hour and a half after lunch. This can have an impact on business as well.

Things in general tend to move slower in Asia. There is not the "hurry hurry" feeling like there is here. There is a definite feeling that if it doesn't get done today there is always tomorrow. The clock is not a major driver in these countries. This can be, and usually is, a real frustration to Americans who want to get things done quickly.

Care needs to be taken when giving compliments. Sometimes compliments can be interpreted as a desire for something. This can make the individual feel that he must give you what you complimented him on, for example, a tie, sweater. There may be a feeling of obligation to give it to you since you are the guest.

MONETARY OR OTHER CONSIDERATIONS

Multiple sources for raw materials are more important on the global level than in the domestic market. Interesting things can happen when the IMF (International Monetary Fund) gets involved, like sudden full deregulation, and so on. This can cause inflation and huge changes in exchange rates. Sometimes countries may not be ready to handle the deregulation and all kinds of difficulties can develop.

Materials may be available internationally that are not available in North America because they are not registered with the proper government agencies here. Care must be taken that regulations in all countries are abided by. An example of this in current times is the REACH initiative that is going on in the European Union now. This is an attempt to have every hazardous chemical that is imported into that area of the world registered and identified with the chemical's use. The importer is the one responsible for the proper filing of the paperwork and paying any of the fees that will be required. It is easy for Americans to look at this and say that it is just another form of tariff. That may be the case but the officials are doing what they feel is best for their countries and we must abide by their desires if we want to continue to do business there.

Other difficulties can be caused by different feedstocks being used in different parts of the world to make similar products, such as natural versus synthetic feedstocks, which are different in their composition.

The ideal situation would be to find a supplier that has manufacturing capabilities around the world using common feedstocks so the same product would be available everywhere.

Reality sometimes falls short of this ideal and compromises must be made. The compromises are determined by what is best for your company at the time. Will slightly different material work in one area and do what is required? Do you need a uniform product around the world?

Global implementation adds a new dimension to the process. It is relatively easy to pick a preferred supplier and move business to them in North America. If you are doing business in Europe, Asia, or even Africa, there are many other factors that can enter the picture. Some of these are:

- Requirements to use products that are manufactured within that country.

- Currency issues in different areas of the world.

- Cultural and relational issues.

- Other business restrictions (imports/exports)

- Capital investments may be necessary to manufacture product within the country.

If operations are being supplied by imports from North America, it will require longer delivery times and thus require the maintenance of higher raw material or product inventory levels. This will tie up working capital. With the focus of many businesses on lean manufacturing and just-in-time inventories some creative results will be required to make this competitive on a global scale.

More and more of the developing nations are requiring that if you intend to do business in their country, you will use materials that are generated in their country. This is an attempt by the various governments to protect the jobs that exist in the country so they can not be eroded by exports.

Currency issues play a very important role. When you are dealing with the local currency many times the net cost will be significantly cheaper than buying something here in North America with U.S. dollars and shipping it to the developing country. As the local economies continue to develop, more and more material may become available locally. Sometimes all the additional costs of buying in North America and shipping can put your required price well above what the market will bear. If this happens, local sourcing will be the only way to compete. The chosen preferred supplier for North America may end up not getting this business if they are unable to manufacture as needed in the specific country.

Another area that needs consideration is the way that age and education are viewed in the Asian culture. Older people are respected and their decisions are the most important. For example, a young American executive is sent to resolve a situation in Asia. If an older Asian were there he might leave and a young person would replace him. If you want to deal with the older leaders, older leaders from America must be there. Meetings can be delayed because of a misunderstanding of this concept. Again, the host country is setting the rules to be abided by and as visitors we must comply with their desires.

Education is much more important in Asia than in the United States. I had workers that wanted to go out of their way to do a good job to please me. Students in Asia are much more interested in doing a good job in their class work. I discovered this as I worked with students in Asia via the Internet. These students were diligent about getting assignments completed on time and correctly. This was an exciting group of students to work with because they had a burning desire to learn and apply what they had learned. This is just about the opposite of what I see in some cases with students in the United States.

Relationships are more important in other cultures than they are here in America. If you are going to sign a contract or close a deal, this can be handled quickly here because all that happens is a paper is signed and the agreement is enforced. When there is a focus on relationships, the other company wants to get to know you and understand a little more about you. This takes time and opportunities must be created for this to happen. You may be shown some tourist attractions, taken to a special dinner or other places just to develop a relationship with the new organization. This takes away the critical time element that exists in North America, where we always feel that we have to get things done right now.

CONCLUSION

By understanding cultural differences you can better do business in other parts of the world. Culture is the underlying structure that determines how things get done in any country. There are many cultural differences and these must be understood to effectively operate in other countries.

KEYWORDS

Culture

Education

Time

Language

DISCUSSION QUESTIONS

1. What are four difficulties that can occur with different cultures?

2. What are "smooth interpersonal relationships"?

3. What problems can smooth interpersonal relationships cause?

4. Is it possible to be shielded from the culture of a country? How?

5. How is the family viewed differently in various cultures?

Continued

Continued

6. What does "yes" mean in various cultures?

7. How is age and status more important in other cultures?

8. Should you always get to a meeting on time?

9. Why would a go-between be used?

10. Are laws uniform around the world? Why not? Give some examples.

8

Building Relationships

An effective relationship with a supplier that covers many areas of business will help reduce the total costs of doing business with that supplier, as well as make sure that the supplier's business is healthy and thus guarantee a supply of needed materials. Relationship-building is time spent that can pay large dividends in the future.

INTRODUCTION

For years upper management would tell the purchasing department to reduce raw material costs by getting suppliers to reduce prices. One of the ways this was accomplished was by basing the bonus paid to the purchasing people on the purchase price variance. The larger the difference (lower), the bigger the bonus paid.

Old management style did not really want a relationship with suppliers. In the global marketplace that exists today, effective relationships with suppliers may be the only way to guarantee a consistent supply of materials needed. An example of this might be when you are dealing with an oil producing country. The supply is based on what OPEC decides and the price is determined by OPEC. A healthy supplier relationship would give a company a higher probability that it would receive some material in a situation like this.

BUILDING A RELATIONSHIP

Two factors are very important to a company's business. The first is to be able to maintain their market share and sell products at a satisfactory profit. The second is to be able to obtain a high quality and guaranteed source for

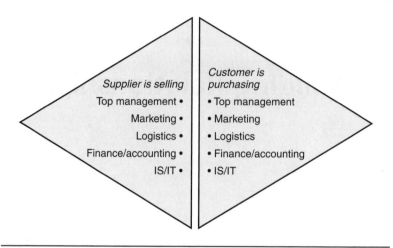

Figure 8.1 The new selling model.

needed materials. These two factors impact each other and have a direct impact on the performance of the business.

One of the first things that must happen in order to begin to have an effective supplier relationship and therefore a consistent supply of raw materials is a paradigm shift. Upper management must understand the potential benefits and be willing to wholeheartedly support the efforts at all levels to make the relationship prosper.

In this new selling model (Figure 8.1) you see the paradigm shift as the two funnels are flipped and contact between the companies is being achieved at all levels of each organization.

All levels in a company need to exercise creative thinking when a supplier is being dealt with. Acceptance of new ideas and changes is a must if a relationship is to grow.

When the supplier has been chosen, then the real work begins as the relationship is built. In business today, we *must* look beyond the "best" price and begin to look at the total cost of doing business with a supplier and how these costs can be reduced. In most areas of business, it is not easy to get good historical data on quality costs. Most quality costs are hidden or not considered a significant cost. Some examples of actions that increase a supplier's costs are:

- Order patterns requiring a supplier to increase their inventory to be able to meet the demand. The supplier needs to be able to predict and schedule production to best service customers and still control business costs. If a company can help in this area with good forecasts, this can be very beneficial for both parties.

- Requirements causing a supplier to make a reserved inventory. This will guarantee that all orders will be met on time and is usually done to eliminate production interruptions due to a sporadic order pattern. The company needs to make better projections in conjunction with the production capability of the supplier.

- On the other hand we can develop problems by ordering small quantities of material to hold our inventory down. A company may be tying up a large reactor to manufacture a little material, incurring increased costs that would offset any inventory costs that would be saved.

- Multiple handling of products. Having the supplier produce and store material and then ship it on demand can be costly to both parties. A forklift can very easily do significant damage to some products.

- Scheduling changes. This is difficult to correct in cyclical businesses, but with good historical data and trending, reasonable consistency that minimizes supplier interruptions can be reached.

- There are so many little things that happen in business every day that cause increased costs. Companies need to be conscious of these and look for ways to reduce them. A company's inflexibility can add costs for the supplier.

In some companies the quality cost picture is displayed as an iceberg with the majority of the cost being hidden under the water level. Finding these hidden costs and making progress at reducing them with suppliers requires a consistent effort. As companies evaluate their suppliers, they find their strengths, and they also find suppliers that are best able to meet their needs and willing to work with them.

The foundation of any relationship has to be trust by both parties. In some cases, as proprietary information will have to be dealt with, secrecy agreements may be necessary. The tone of a relationship is usually set at the time of the initial negotiations. Negotiations must not be approached with a "give me" attitude only. A company must put the supplier in a "win–win" situation as well as themselves. The supplier must be placed in a position where he gets a reasonable profit from the business since the supplier wants to remain in business and so does the company. Remember, the indications of the verbal agreements are the intentions that a company should abide by when dealing with its suppliers. The legal contracts can get very difficult to understand.

As relationships with suppliers are developed, creativity needs to be applied so new areas can be explored. Some new areas might be:

- Top executives meeting and becoming friends and really supporting the relationship. A way to do this might be to have an outing where they get together in an informal setting and can become friends while they learn the strengths of both companies and what they can accomplish together. This should be done at least once a year. Perhaps the expense can be shared or the outing rotated from supplier to company.

- Share technical expertise through seminars. This could be set up to be done monthly by rotating different suppliers. Most suppliers are more than willing to make a several-hour presentation two times a year. This keeps the technical departments in the company up to date with the things that the supplier is working on. Continuing education for technical disciplines can be hard to find for specific areas and suppliers can become a real resource.

- Have technical people from both companies meet face to face (develop friendships). This also produces contacts within the technical community. When difficult situations develop and an answer or recommendation is needed, a friend in the suppliers' laboratory can be an asset in quickly resolving the situation.

- Share end uses with the supplier so they better understand where their material is being used. Production workers enjoy knowing where their products end up and what they are being used for. A short description of these products and their uses can make a supplier's employees have a better feeling about their work and what they are making.

- Train employees from both organizations by using each company's resources to help both grow. There are often common training requirements that the government has defined as well as some that are just beneficial. The common training could be shared, reducing the duplication of a lot of dollars. Some examples might be RCRA training, hazardous waste training, or Hazwoper 40-hour training. These are just a few of the common ones that are required today.

- Team members from both companies meet on a regular basis (quarterly or semiannually) to discuss what is going right and what could be done better. Here problems that have been resolved as well as the sore spots that remain can be placed on the table and openly discussed and resolved. This must be done if the relationship is to continue to grow.

- Share analytical equipment, technicians, and methods. Special laboratory equipment can cost a lot of money and in some cases is not continually used. Specialized equipment purchases can be shared and both companies can reap the benefits of the equipment. A specific example of this would be an NMR spectrometer or a cyclical salt spray apparatus.

- Ask the question: What else can this supplier do for me? Be creative and get out of the old mold. Ask the question and see where the answer leads. A company may never know what could happen until they explore the possibilities.

- Look for unusual possibilities for working together. For example:

  - *Use of suppliers' byproducts.* Does the supplier have a byproduct that the company is trying to buy on the market? If it is not up to the specifications required, what would it take to get it there? This could be costing the supplier disposal costs as well. A match here could have a real financial impact quickly.

  - *Common raw material sourcing.* In some cases very similar materials are used by both companies. Maybe the one with the larger need could increase their volume so that both benefit on the larger volume leverage.

  - *Share equipment.* Idle equipment is a significant hidden cost. Does a supplier have extra capacity that can be used to help the company and decrease the overall cost of the plant?

  - *Creative inventory management.* Some areas to investigate here may be supplier managed inventory or receiving in larger quantities on a consignment basis and helping a supplier with a warehouse in the area.

  - *Creative logistics.* Developing the company's own or supplier's delivery system can be very cost-effective for both companies.

Each discipline in the company has a different perspective. By visiting each others' sites, different disciplines will see different opportunities. These opportunities need to be explored to see if both parties could benefit from them.

Remember, relationships do not just happen, they take work and time to develop. Work at it!

MEASUREMENT OF SUCCESS

As a result of building relationships, the role of the purchasing department will change from being concerned about pricing to managing the suppliers. Managing suppliers requires that methods be put in place to show how both parties are doing. A simple way to do this is by the use of a scorecard that is filled out each month dealing with the critical points of the business. This creates a baseline so improvements can be measured. This scorecard will vary from industry to industry and probably from company to company as priorities vary. Late or early shipments are very important in JIT (just in time) environments. If a company is dealing with a bulk shipment to a storage tank, all they want is it to be there before they run out. If scores are kept, a progress rating can be seen as both processes improve. It can be a measuring stick, as well as a pat on the back for a job well done. By working with fewer suppliers, it becomes easier to keep in touch with and deal with them all. The adversarial attitudes will not exist in a true relationship. Friends want to help friends do better! Remember, building relationships is a process where both suppliers and customers will be growing together.

At first it will be difficult to put together the savings, but as we grow, the changes will be able to be converted into dollars. This is when even greater commitment of upper management can be secured. Remember, upper management speaks in dollars. "What am I getting for this money?" We need to answer this question and be able to document the savings by increasing profits.

Another consideration that must be handled in a relationship is who gets any savings. In a solid relationship greed does not exist. A very effective way to divide the savings is to give one-third to the supplier, one-third to the company, and one-third to the customer. By using this type of division, any process improvements all the way down the line benefit the customer, which will help solidify market share. If a company does not pass savings along to the customer, the risk is that a competitor will, and significant market share could be lost.

QUESTIONS FOR CONSIDERATION

Is it really safe to sole-source my raw materials? I would answer this question by asking how serious you are about forming a relationship with your supplier. If this question is answered in the affirmative, then you will both have contingency plans that will work for each other.

What should I do if I go out and bid products, just to see if my suppliers are staying in line with market pricing, and I get lower prices? The first thing you must be aware of is that the suppliers who lost business are going to want it back. They may even be willing to lowball the pricing to try to get it back. If a company falls for this trap, they are back to doing things the old way, based on price only. They should meet with the preferred supplier and discuss the situation. In many cases, the price may be dealt with here. As the relationship grows and the costs of both of the companies are understood, it may not be necessary for a meeting.

Should I keep in touch with other suppliers? The other suppliers need to be kept in touch with for several reasons. The primary reason is that new technology needs to be used to keep a company on the cutting edge. New things need to be shared with the technical groups.

Is requiring our suppliers to be certified to ISO 9001 good enough? ISO 9001 creates a good quality system and starting point. The simplified definition that has been given is to "Say what you do and do what you say." Continuous improvement goes beyond this and looks at better ways of doing things. Every process needs to continually get better.

A small supplier may look at ISO 9001 as an overburdening expense for what they will receive. Effective relationships can help overcome the negatives and small companies can become certified and still remain healthy suppliers.

OVERCOMING BARRIERS

Obstacles exist in some management styles that can inhibit or destroy relationship-building. Some of these are:

- Old-style managers. Supportive upper management is a must if the relationships are to develop since some travel and money will be involved.

- Plant purchasing people. Previously we have asked them to make sure that they can get any of our raw materials whenever we need them. In order to guarantee the supply, several suppliers' products had to be accessible. Over time, friendships developed with these suppliers' reps. These friendships may be difficult to break. It will take work to bring the purchasing agent into the sole-source supplier mind-set.

- Research and development people need to begin to make the preferred supplier their choice. Old habits die slow! Suppliers from previous jobs may be hard to eliminate.

- Desire for the status quo by either company needs to be removed so problems can be solved at their root and everyone can get beyond dealing only with symptoms.

- History has to be placed on the table and dealt with so a new page can be turned. Old problems must not be brought up over and over once they have been dealt with. We need to deal with today's situations.

THE IDEAL SITUATION

As noted in *Lean Thinking* by James Womack, the ideal, lowest-cost situation is where the entire supply chain operates with no inventory, and parts or product are made to order. Companies need to do everything they can to approach this ideal to remove costs from the system. As the ideal is approached, the delivery time of products can be improved and the quality of the products will also improve.

Most companies today believe that making more products faster is the best way to reduce costs. Operating in this mode can build a significant inventory of unneeded material and tie up large amounts of working capital.

The paradigm shift required is to begin to examine the entire supply chain and look at reducing inventories to zero. This will require changes at all levels of business from the boardroom all the way to the factory floor. Effective supplier relationships are the only way to begin to make this happen.

TWO REAL APPLICATIONS

In our first scenario, when a company has grown by acquisition, the result is often many suppliers of the same types of products. Preferred suppliers need to be selected and product orders moved to those suppliers. This should be done as soon as possible. The new company will see several advantages working with a preferred supplier. One advantage is increased volume to the selected supplier, thus giving the company more leverage. This leverage helps in future price negotiations. Another advantage is that five suppliers versus more than twenty suppliers are much easier to manage. It is a lot easier to deal with any quality issues and get them resolved. As these relationships continue to grow, costs are eliminated for both companies.

The second application occurred when I was dealing with a customer of Carbon Pitch. This customer wanted us to do SQC (statistical quality control) to guarantee the quality of pitch at their facilities. As the relationship begins, a company should not ask the supplier to do things for them that they are not willing to do themselves. For example, what does it accomplish for a company to have the supplier providing SPC (statistical process control) or SQC data when the company does not do either themselves? All that will happen is data collection. Data needs to be useful in order to help the relationship improve for both parties. This was a real education process for both of us as we had to learn as we went along what really impacted the quality of this material. We ran 10 different tests on each batch and our internal specifications covered them all. When the customer received the material, they sampled it and ran only two tests. We were providing them with the results of most of our 10 tests.

The solution was to have meetings between the management of both companies where the performance of our pitch and its impact on their plants' performance were discussed. The group met, and with two overhead projectors put up SPC data that had been collected by both companies for the same time period. The blips were discussed by both parties. This required a very detailed understanding of the processes by both parties, but a lot of money can be saved with this level of understanding. As a result of these meetings a much clearer understanding of both processes developed. A company needs to understand their process and how it impacts both their customers and suppliers. Many times the critical parameters are not the ones being measured. Another result of these meetings was that the customer decided to accept our analysis and control charts rather than waiting for their analysis to be done. This resulted in one less lab technician and reduced the inventory on site by 25 to 50 percent. As a supplier, we were better able to manage a consistent order pattern.

Patience and determination are needed to resolve problems and gain understanding. Data for data's sake is not a good idea. Suppliers may run many more tests than their customer receives results for, but the customer really does not want all the data. They want only the data that impacts their process.

CONCLUSION

Taking the time to investigate and select a supplier can provide a good preferred supplier. Building a relationship with that supplier is what makes an excellent supplier.

If an excellent supplier is not found, it must be developed!

KEYWORDS

Relationships

Possibilities

Savings

Obstacles

Costs

Total cost of doing business

Price

Sole-sourcing

DISCUSSION QUESTIONS

1. How can costs be added to a supplier's process by our actions?

2. What are some new areas that should be considered in supplier relationships?

3. What are some unusual possibilities that should be considered in supplier relationships?

4. How should savings from process changes be divided in supplier relationships?

5. What is sole-sourcing?

6. What is a method that can be used to verify that the price that you are paying for a material or service is in line with the market rate?

7. What method or methods can be used to identify new technology in the supply chain?

8. What type of quality system should be implemented in a good relationship atmosphere?

9. What are some obstacles that may need to be overcome in supplier relationships?

9

Supplier Quality System Surveys, Visits, and Continuous Improvement

T he development of supplier surveys and planning supplier visits are two methods that can help improve the relationship with and understanding of the supplier. Better understanding the supplier reveals strengths and weaknesses, and both organizations can be improved as the strengths are built upon.

SUPPLIER QUALITY SYSTEM SURVEYS

The purpose of this survey is to gain an understanding of the quality system that is in place or in progress at the supplier. The survey can be used as documentation of the quality system status of each supplier. Some of the things that can be learned from a survey of the supplier are:

Do they have a third-party registration to a quality standard?

Are they planning on seeking a registration to a quality standard?

Survey Development

The survey can be very detailed or very basic. The issue is, what type of information are you really interested in? Surveys can be short or in some cases very lengthy. The one concept to remember is that the longer the survey, the less likely that you will get a response. The benefits of a short, very specific survey are:

- You will get the information you need.

- It will not be time-consuming for the supplier.

- One sheet of paper can be used.

- The turnaround with the completed results will be faster.

Supplier Quality System Survey

Questionnaire for ISO 9001 Quality System Requirements

		Yes	No
Supplier name			
Supplier address			
		Yes	No
Do you have knowledge of ISO 9001?			
Are you third-party registered?	ISO 9001		
	ISO/TS 16949		
Are you a tier 1 supplier to the Big Three? (GM, Ford, Chrysler)			
Are you pursuing third-party registration?			
If so, when?			
And with whom?			
Completed by		Date	
Title		Phone #	
Please return with a copy of your registration (if available) by mail or fax to Attn: Office manager			

Figure 9.1 Sample supplier quality system survey.

When a survey is being developed about the quality system, you need to consider what parts of the system are you interested in. If you want to know everything about the system you are going to create a long survey and may not get the information that you need.

A sample of a simple quality system survey is shown as Figure 9.1.

This survey collects the essential information that is needed about the organization's quality system and what is in store in the future. It is short and very easy to fill out.

SUPPLIER VISITS

Several things need to be addressed as a supplier visit is being planned. The first things to decide are what the purpose of the visit is and who from your organization will be going on it. A defined purpose for the visit will suggest the people that should be involved in the visit. Remember that more than three or four people may intimidate the supplier, and they may not feel comfortable even with that many people depending on the size of the supplier. The supplier will have to be the one to suggest the dates and be involved in the planning from their end. The supplier should be contacted and made aware of the purpose of the visit and which positions from your company will be represented. This allows the supplier to make sure that the comparable people from their company can be available for the visit. If you feel you need specific people available during the visit, they should be requested early in the planning stages so that arrangements can be made for their presence. Remember, a well planned visit always works out better than an unplanned visit.

There are five things that need to be completed before the actual visit. They are:

1. Review any problems or issues that have occurred with the supplier so that you can observe whether they have been fixed.

2. Understand your requirements so that you are able to help correct any misunderstandings that the supplier has.

3. Be prepared to explain challenges that are created at your facilities when changes are made (what went wrong and how it is impacting the overall business).

4. Realize that an aggressive attitude like "I'm right and you had better do it my way" is unproductive.

5. Create measurables that are important to your business for a particular commodity or product and share them with the supplier.

The following are factors that need to be considered and/or reviewed at the visit (adjusted and expanded from *Supply Chain Management: Strategy, Planning, and Operations* by Chopra and Meindel).

Replenishment Lead Time

This is how long it takes for an order of material to arrive. The longer the lead time, the larger the inventory that will be required. As you visit a supplier you will be able to observe the size of the inventories of both raw materials and finished goods. This is a good point of departure for discussion to see if any actions are being taken to reduce lead time and what these actions are.

On-Time Performance

This measure can be defined by different companies in different ways. For example, in one organization any shipments that are received early are considered on time. In another company as long as part of the shipment is on time the entire order is considered on time. In another case if the shipment is within one day early or late it is considered on time. As you can see, one of the first issues that must to be discussed is the supplier's definition of on time and your definition of on time to make sure that they are the same. A difference in definition can cause some real problems with data that is being shared and interpreted by two different organizations.

Supply Flexibility

This describes how much the capacity for a product is able to vary with the supplier in a given time frame. This gives an indication of the capability of the supplier to handle your needs if they change significantly in a given time frame. The goal should be to have a supplier that has enough flexibility to be able to meet the wildest swings in your demand. This may be hard to find, but some negotiations and trade-offs may be able to be made.

Delivery Frequency/Minimum Lot Size

This factor deals with minimum quantities that can be produced as well as smaller, more frequent deliveries. By being able to deliver smaller quantities more frequently the supplier can reduce inventory costs for both companies. A discussion of how this is accomplished or how this can be accomplished can be held while at the supplier's site.

Supply Quality

These requirements are the expectations both written and unwritten of the customer. The supplier needs to understand both of them and be able to meet them. The quality characteristics and tolerances that are defined need to be realistic with respect to the requirements so that the supplier is able to compete and supply the product that is really needed. I have seen engineers pull specifications and tolerances from the air under the assumption that the narrower they are the better the product will be and the probability of receiving a bad product will be less. This is bad because the tighter the specification, the more costly the operations at the supplier will be. I have seen overprocessing specified in this manner and the engineers could not see the additional costs that they were causing because of the way the product had been specified.

Inbound Transportation Costs

Today there are many different ways to ship products around the world and some are more expensive than others. An evaluation of transportation methods needs to be completed to see what would be the best for both companies. Sometimes this may be a combination of several methods. I was involved in a situation where material was coming in from Japan as a liquid. It had to be transferred to a barge in the Gulf of Mexico and pushed up the Mississippi River to a port where the barge was unloaded into trucks and taken to the final destination. There are many types of containers that are available today of various sizes when ocean freight has to be used.

Pricing Terms

This is probably the least important of all the factors. This is a factor that is negotiable where the other factors are not. The price and terms need to be acceptable for both parties, and it must be remembered that the supplier has to be able to make a profit in order to remain healthy.

Information Coordination Capability

This is where the electronic capabilities of the organizations are discussed. Are the orders posted to a Web site on the Internet where the supplier is required to go and get them and then fulfill this demand, or are other electronic means used? Fax and e-mail can also be used to transmit orders and information between companies. One of the latest trends is the use of electronic transfer of funds. This has been facilitated by using bar codes on incoming materials, which are scanned in and when the proper amount is received, payment is made to the supplier electronically. By using this technology a large amount of paperwork and costs have been removed from the processes and both organizations benefit.

Design Collaboration Capability

Depending on the requirements of the customer, this may be a critical area for the supplier. Many times the supplier has more experience and ability to help design the product than the customer themselves. Is the supplier willing to share and help in this area? That depends on the benefits that the customer is willing to provide. The customer can make sure that this supplier gets a majority of the projects for design and development, and perhaps they may be given the production phase as well. There has to be a benefit for both parties for this to work.

Exchange Rates, Taxes, and Duties

These factors enter in significantly when the supplier is international and may not be using U.S. currency for payment. There may also be limits as far as volumes that increase taxes and duties. All of this needs to be considered with the supplier. When material is coming through customs there can be delays and as a result deliveries may be missed or late. I have seen projected dates missed as containers were held in customs for an extra day or two. A good relationship with the supplier may help work through some of these issues and make adjustments.

Supplier Viability

A supplier has to be healthy and making a profit in order to remain in business. Another area that must be examined is working capital. If accounts receivable are not being paid in a timely manner the company could run out of cash and have to file for bankruptcy. When discussing the financial situation of an organization there are many areas that need to be looked at. Cash on hand, profitability, accounts receivable, and how long it takes to get paid are several of the important factors that need to be discussed with the supplier.

Quoted Price

Again this may be a negotiable figure because price is what determines the profit and viability of the organization. It is easy to make the supplier stick to the quoted price but it must be remembered that changes may cost money and make the product a nonprofitable item for the supplier that could then be discontinued. Care needs to be taken in this area so that a supply of material will remain available.

Late Deliveries

This is a term that needs to be defined specifically so that the supplier knows your expectations. Included in the definition should be what happens in the event of a late delivery. For example, is the shipment rejected? Any other penalties that will be imposed on the supplier need to be defined.

Premium Freight

This can be a very expensive process to meet the customer's needs. A definition of expectations must be developed and shared with the supplier so that the supplier understands when and what type of premium freight should be used. I have seen companies spend a tremendous amount of money flying parts in via helicopter to meet the customer's need. By doing this the supplier may be putting their own business in jeopardy because of the additional costs that are being incurred. This is where companies need to be honest with suppliers and work with them to help keep costs out of the supply chain.

Shipping Damage

When this happens products are lost or can create production problems. Where the customer's responsibility for the product begins is usually defined by the purchase order, but many times not everyone in both organizations is aware of where the responsibility changes hands. For example, it can be considered the customer's property as soon as it leaves the supplier's plant or it may remain the responsibility of the supplier until it arrives at the customer's facility.

Quality-Related Returns

These have to be handled individually so that both parties have a chance to understand and resolve any issues. It is my recommendation that if there is a complaint or a product issue, you need to see the actual product so that you are able to test and verify the situation. Doing this makes discussion development a little easier once an analysis has been done. By having the product in hand, many times the operation that caused the problem can be identified and the problem fixed in a timely manner.

Performing the Visit

The preferred way to do a supplier visit is to meet their people in a conference room and give the supplier a chance to showcase their business and their strengths. This can take as much as one to two hours depending on what the supplier desires to present. In my experience I have seen notebooks prepared with lots of information about the organization and what they desire the customer to know. Doing this allows the information to get back to the customer and they are not relying on the note-taking capabilities of the people performing the visit. This allows the information that the supplier desires to share to be correctly presented. In this part of the visit you will begin to get a sense of the supplier's desire to be a supplier to your organization. As the meeting goes on you should be able to have some open discussions as to problems caused by different actions by the supplier. As a customer you should be listening carefully to what the supplier is presenting for you. They have put a significant effort into this visit and respect for their efforts needs to be shown. As you have questions, you need to write these down and note important issues that come to mind. These will help you to remember when the discussion time arrives.

A major part of the preparation should be learning as much as possible about the plant or company that you are going to visit before the actual visit. This will require research to find out if any specific issues exist. The research should include any issues that have been created for your organization as a result of the behavior of the supplier. The time frame that would be covered by the research could be several years to get enough data to create a healthy discussion and make sure the incident is not an isolated occasion. Remember, the idea is to help the supplier get better and not to get into an argument about what may be trivial issues. Reviewing any problems that have been encountered with the supplier and the solutions that were offered provides a base for a good discussion later on the day of the visit.

One of the major parts of a supplier visit should be a plant tour. As you are going on the tour be sure to write down comments or questions that you would like to have explained later. The plant tour should start at the beginning of the operation (usually receiving), proceed through the operations, and finish at the shipping area. By doing the tour this way, inefficiencies along the way may be exposed and can be discussed later. While on the tour you should be looking around as you walk through the facility observing:

- Is the facility clean and orderly?

- Do you observe a systematic flow of product through their process?

- Ask employees questions and see if they understand their job.

- Is receiving inspection used?

- How is the process monitored?

- What happens to bad parts?

- How is rework handled?

- What is involved in final inspection?

- Observe the operations—what do you see?

- What type of storage facilities are available for raw materials as well as finished goods?

- How is the inventory managed?

- Do they have a large inventory?

- Is there an indication of good supplier relationships with their suppliers?

- What kinds of technology do you observe?

- Do you see work instructions posted at the job sites?

- How are incoming materials labeled?

- If you see research and development, is the focus of new technology in your product area?

- Did you observe any other products that this supplier may be able to provide for you?

- As you observe the equipment being used, imagine how this will fit into any of your outsourcing needs.

The plant tour should also take from one to two hours or longer depending on the size of the facility. For example, a small injection molding facility would require less time than a diesel engine assembly plant. It has been my experience that the critical part of the visit is the plant tour, and by doing this correctly many improvements at both facilities can be realized. I have had research and development facilities included at the beginning of a visit so that this part of the business becomes visible to the customer, and to show what steps are being taken to make sure current technologies are being used and new ones are being developed. By doing this the customer can see the real focus of the supplier's business. I had a supplier of surfactants for cleaning products that was focused on the plastics business, and this piece of the business was acquired as part of a plastics acquisition. It was not a primary focus of the business and it was hard for them to even effectively discuss the surfactants business.

The measurables that were developed earlier in the process need to be observed as you are walking through the facility. Look for things that can impact the measurable in both positive and negative ways so that constructive comments can be made later during the discussion. Do not hesitate to ask questions as you are going on the plant tour. This may be the exact place to get some of your questions or concerns answered. Remember to record the answers if they are important for the visit so that they will appear in the final report.

Discussion Time

This is the time after the plant tour where both groups are back in the conference room. Questions should be posed and answers given and a better understanding of both organizations should begin here. Some questions need to be discussed in the following areas: cost, delivery, quality, and environmental. Some of the questions might be:

Cost

- Do you have a cost of quality system?
- How do you measure scrap?
- How do you value scrap?
- How is rework handled?
- Is Six Sigma being used?
- What type of relationship do you have with your suppliers?
- What arrangements have been put in place to guarantee a continuous supply of material in case of a catastrophic event?

Delivery

- What logistical suppliers are used?
- What kind of relationship is maintained with these suppliers?
- What type of accountability system is in place?

Quality

- What are their expectations versus yours?
- How do they ensure quality material?
- Do they use incoming inspection?
- Do they use SPC? Where and on which processes?
- What type of quality system training has been done?
- Do they have and maintain a registered quality system?
- Who is their registrar?
- What types of nonconformances have been found in internal and external audits?

Environmental

- Do you have an environmental management system in place?
- Is it registered to ISO 14001?

- Are there any major environmental issues facing your company at present?

In the remaining time you will need to:

- Ask any questions remaining from the supplier presentation or the plant tour.

- Clarify any inconsistencies that you feel exist.

- Ask how they see your company as a customer. What type of issues do they have? This allows the supplier to share their views with you. With the changes that are going on in the market today, this can give you an idea of how you are viewed by the supplier. As more and more customers are being rationalized, it is very useful to know where you are perceived in this potential process.

Reporting the Visit Results

At the end of the visit a meeting with the supplier's people should reconvene in the conference room. This time the customer again explains what they were looking for and what their observations were and what their recommendations will be. The supplier needs to be given a chance for rebuttal because things could have been missed or misinterpreted. This is the point where everything is reviewed and agreed on. There should be *no* surprises for the supplier after the visit. This should be handled just like the results of an audit, because that is what it could be considered.

A report should be developed that summarizes the visit. This report should contain comments about the answers to questions and observations, and the results and recommendations that will be made. Copies of this report should be sent to all of those in attendance at the visit as well as any other people that need copies in both organizations. Meetings can be set up to discuss the results and further actions based on the report but there should be no surprises for the supplier as a result of the visit.

CONTINUOUS IMPROVEMENT METHODS

Corrective Action

A corrective action system should be in place at the supplier's location. One of the main benefits of a corrective action system is that it identifies problems and drives solutions so that the problem will not happen again. This is a process that needs to be managed and communicated to the suppliers. I have seen organizations that require a response to a corrective action within 48 hours and a complete review completed and posted to a Web site within 14 days. If this type of process is used, a feedback system needs to be put in place that will help the supplier understand what is expected so that a lot of quick solutions do not get posted to the Web. I have seen a weakness in this area when the supplier does not receive any feedback and as a result they have no real desire to do a detailed review to really benefit from the process.

Root Cause Analysis

This is a process that identifies the real cause of a problem. Once it is identified, changes can be made and the problem should not happen again. There are many ways to identify the root cause of a problem. These will be discussed in Chapter 12 on applying basic quality tools to suppliers and customers.

CONCLUSION

With the proper planning and preparation, an excellent supplier quality system survey can be developed and suppliers will fill it out and return it in a timely manner. The same is true for the preparation for a supplier visit. If the preparations are completed and the visit is conducted with an open mind, some very positive results can be obtained for both organizations. Continuous improvement is a necessity for businesses today to be able to remain in a competitive position. Part of continuous improvement is doing root cause analysis of problem areas to prevent the problems from happening again.

KEYWORDS

Supplier quality system survey

Continuous improvement

Supplier visit

Root cause analysis

DISCUSSION QUESTIONS

1. Why would you want a survey of a supplier's quality system?

2. Name some things that can be learned from a supplier quality system survey.

3. What are some issues that might create a need for a supplier visit?

4. What are areas that questions need to focus on while visiting a supplier?

5. Why is it important to identify the root cause of a problem and correct it?

6. What measurables could be used for a supplier?

7. How do supplier visits fit into a supply chain management process?

8. What are the benefits of a very short supplier survey?

9. What five things should be completed before a supplier visit?

10. What should you be observing on the plant tour?

11. What are some of the factors that should be considered and reviewed at the supplier visit?

12. How does corrective action indicate continuous improvement?

13. What are some questions that could be asked about costs and delivery?

14. What are some questions that could be asked about quality and environmental concerns?

10

Supplier Scorecards and Measures

Today we are competing in a global economy. The days when we could focus on the domestic economy are gone. This is very evident when we realize that as a consumer today there are three things that are desired. They are: world-class quality, fast delivery, and the best possible price. None of these desires holds any indication about where it is made. As long as all three of these desires can be met, the consumer will be happy.

The implications of the globalization of the supply chain require both customers and suppliers in many different businesses to rethink and change their processes of doing business.

We will need to develop scorecards and measures for suppliers because the quality standards require it. For example, the standard ISO 9001:2000 states the following in Section 7.4.1, Purchasing Process:

> The organization shall evaluate and select suppliers based on their ability to supply product in accordance with the organization's requirements. Criteria for selection, evaluation and re-evaluation shall be established. Records of the results of evaluations and any necessary actions arising from the evaluation shall be maintained.

The standard ISO/TS 16949:2002 states in Section 7.4.3.2, Supplier Monitoring:

> Supplier Performance shall be monitored through the following indicators:
>
> - Delivered product quality
>
> - Customer disruptions including field returns
>
> - Delivery schedule performance (including incidents of premium freight)

- Special status customer notifications related to quality or delivery issues.

The organization shall promote supplier monitoring of the performance of their manufacturing processes.

Three of the old measures used to evaluate suppliers were cost, delivery, and quality. Quality is measured as parts per million (PPM) defective and is reported to the supplier on a regular basis. Delivery is based on materials being received on time. The number of shipments is used for the measurement in this area. Price is what was agreed to in the contract. In most cases this is the cheapest one. These were good measures, but as competition gets stronger we will need to get better and our measures will have to change.

One of the possibilities is a concept called *total perfect order.* My definition of a total perfect order is meeting the following:

- Right time

- Right amount

- Right place

- Right paperwork

- Right price

- Right quality

- Right shipper

If all of these characteristics are met we will have a perfect order.

Let's begin by looking at *right time:* when the customer wants it. Some questions that need to be answered are:

- Does the customer give you a specific window for a delivery?

- What happens if the shipment is early or late?

- Should we have to use premium freight?

With the answers to these questions a better understanding of the customer requirements is available and can be acted on by the supplier.

Let's look at *right amount:* how many pieces the customer wants. Some questions that need to be answered are:

- What impact does overshipping have on the customer?

- What impact does back-ordering have on the customer?

With these questions answered the customer requirements and impacts will be understood.

Overshipping can create a variety of different problems. For example, let's assume that a hospital ordered 1000 hypodermic needles. The supplier made 1005 but these extra needles are not useful to the supplier so they are sent with the order. What will the customer do? There are four options for the customer:

1. Reject the entire order and return it to the supplier. If this is a product that is needed now, the hospital will run out of the needed material.

2. Return the five needles that are over. This shows the supplier that you want what you ask for.

3. Accept the shipment as is and use the needles that came in. Since it is an item that gets regularly used this may be an option.

4. Look at the invoice and only pay for what was ordered even if the bill was also for the extra material shipped. Again this shows the supplier that you want just what you have ordered.

These four options are available when the material arrives and a decision has to be made by the customer as to which action is going to be taken.

The next issue becomes back orders. Are they allowed and how long a time is acceptable to the customer? These are important issues that need to be understood and communicated between the customer and supplier.

Let's look at *right place:* where the customer wants it. The worst scenario here would be a wrong address, but what about a delivery to a company that has 25 loading docks? Do we need to specify the dock location to get the material where the customer wants it? In companies that have many docks, it is easy to lose materials or send them to the wrong place. I have had calls that materials were never delivered only to find out that they had been moved to another location in the customer's warehouse unbeknownst to the individual calling. Bar codes are being used more and more on shipments today so that when the material arrives the bar code can be scanned and the material and purchase order can be matched. This helps speed up operations as well as payment for the goods.

Let's look at *right paperwork:* what the customer requires as well as any regulatory requirements.

In the chemical industry most companies will require a certificate of analysis (COA) for each shipment. Chemicals are supposed to have a Material Safety Data Sheet with each shipment. In the metals industry they use a similar method with customer tests, typically called a material certification. Packing slips accompany most orders, regardless of industry type.

Some customers may require that statistical process control (SPC) data or other statistical data be provided with each shipment. This is a way to get more detailed manufacturing information and look at process variability during the manufacturing process.

Questions that need to be considered are:

- What happens if the right information is not with the shipment?

- What will the response of the customer be?

The shipment could be rejected depending on the importance of the paperwork. In some instances where the papers have legal ramifications, the load will *have* to be rejected.

Let's look at *right price:* negotiated by the customer's purchasing department and the supplier's sales department. Some questions that need to be considered are:

- What happens when an incorrect price is placed on an invoice?

- What extra effort must be made to correct the issue in both companies?

- Does it make either organization happy?

- How important is price in your organization?

These questions will give some indication of what happens when mistakes are made and some of the responses that will be seen.

Let's look at *right quality:* the level the customer wants or better if possible. Most customers want zero defects. The traditional method was to use a random sample and develop an acceptable quality level (AQL). A sampling plan was developed and then the sampling standard tables were looked at to determine if the lot should be accepted or rejected. Using the acceptable quality level indicated that the customer was willing to accept some defects. In most cases today this method is not used. With the advent of Six Sigma the levels of acceptability have come way down, approaching zero defects.

A question that needs to be understood is:

- What happens at the customer's facility if a supplier supplies a bad or defective part or material?

Part of building a relationship will involve gaining an understanding of the impact that bad material has on the customer's process. This may give an indication of where the supplier needs to implement process controls to prevent making defects.

Let's look at *right shipper:* how the customer wants the supplier to get the material to them. As logistics management becomes more prevalent as part of supply chain management, more and more companies will be negotiating contracts with logistics companies for handling inbound and outbound materials from facilities. Companies are beginning to specify the trucking companies that are to be used to ship the supplier's products to them. This is where a supplier has an opportunity to develop a good relationship with logistics companies that in the past may have been ignored as not being a part of the supply chain.

Now let's look at how these measurables may appear on a scorecard. The scorecard is shown in Figure 10.1.

As each order is handled in the process, this scorecard can be used to compile the results for each supplier. As an order is completed the following questions are answered:

- Was the order delivered on time?

- Was the right amount shipped?

- Did the order go to the right place?

- Did the right paperwork accompany the order?

- Did the right price get billed?

- Was the quality of the product correct?

- Was the correct shipper used?

- Were all seven criteria met?

For each question answered affirmatively a tick mark can be placed in the number portion of the scorecard. A tick mark gets entered into the total column as well for each order. At the end of the time cycle being used, monthly, quarterly, and so on, the percentages can be calculated. As the percentages are evaluated and discussed, areas for improvement will become evident and projects can be developed and worked on in these areas.

I have seen many organizations use the three measureables mentioned earlier and be able to successfully deliver orders on time, and with the correct quality and price.

	Time	Amount	Place	Paper work	Price	Quality	Shipper	Perfect	Total
Number									
Percent									

Percent is (number/total number) × 100

Figure 10.1 Total perfect order scorecard.

By using a measure like total perfect orders to evaluate the performance of suppliers, you are able to get a complete picture of their performance. Most suppliers get most of the criteria right for an order, but the focus needs to be on getting all seven of the criteria right. Performance like this is what it is going to take to remain competitive in the global market.

An interesting exercise is to take a look at even the past month and see how your performance would change using the new measurable of total perfect orders.

Suppliers have to be financially healthy and make a reasonable return for their efforts. Customers can not continue to just demand a lower and lower price so they can be competitive. Efforts need to be taken to work with suppliers to make sure they are healthy and will be around to supply products in the future. An example of what can happen if we do not take care of suppliers is what is going on with the tier one and tier two suppliers to the Big Three automotive companies. A significant number of these have been forced to file for Chapter 11 bankruptcy protection. This is not a healthy situation for the entire supply chain.

The transplant auto companies like Honda and Toyota keep supplier performance records, but if a problem develops they are willing to come and help resolve the situation. They do not just come and attack and demand that the problem be resolved like the Big Three automakers do.

The PPM performance is what is used to determine quality level performance in many current systems. This is only one of the measures of the total perfect order. There can be undetected hidden costs at the supplier if you rely on one specific measure. As a supplier, if I know I have trouble with a process, I could be sorting or reinspecting material several times to make sure the PPM numbers look good. This is really not a good answer as it is adding costs to the process that someone has to cover.

Let's look at delivery performance. The customer may be looking at on-time deliveries, which separates out only those that are late. Two things can occur, first material is received early, which creates a storage problem for the customer as well as increasing the possibility of material being damaged or lost. Secondly, the supplier may be using expedited carriers and paying premium freight costs. Both of these may look good at the customer end, but in reality they are adding significantly to the costs of the supplier and reducing the profit margin of the supplier.

The final measure being used is price. This needs to be agreed upon but it should not be expected to be reduced every year without help to improve the suppler's producing process. Supplier development is an important issue in removing costs from the supply chain. It must be accomplished in a manner that will make both the customer and the supplier better. Sometimes I see this being done by customers telling the suppliers they want a 10 percent reduction next year. This type of approach can very easily put the supplier in an unhealthy position and potentially put the customer's supply base at risk.

If the seven requirements of the total perfect order model are met, the process should be functioning like a well-oiled machine. What I typically find is that the percentage of total perfect orders is very low because at least one area gets messed up.

One way to begin the process is to build a scorecard for each supplier, or it can even be used as a measure for your own company's performance as well. The scorecard could be set up and updated monthly.

CONCLUSION

As you can see, many of these measureables are *what, where, when, how,* and *how many*. The *who* is the supplier's company and the *why* is because the supplier and the customer desire to generate a profit so that both organizations are able to remain in business.

The scorecard should be filled out by both the company's customers and their suppliers. These results need to be analyzed and compared. This can give an indication of how an organization is performing at both the customer and supplier levels. When this is accomplished, customer needs that are not clear will be able to be clarified and improvements can be made. Cross-functional teams can be used between the two organizations to help improve both companies' processes. The frequency of the meetings should be determined by business volume and the needs of the customer organization.

KEYWORDS

Right time

Right amount

Right place

Right paperwork

Right price

Right quality

Continued

Continued

Right shipper

Total perfect order

Monitoring

Measureables

DISCUSSION QUESTIONS

1. Why should a supplier be monitored?

2. What type of measureables can be used to monitor a supplier?

3. What is a total perfect order?

4. How do the quality standards require monitoring of suppliers?

5. Will the same scorecard work for different industries? Why?

6. How can the scorecard be used as a continuous improvement tool?

7. Name two standards that have statements about supplier requirements.

8. What are the three old supplier measures?

9. What are the seven parts of the total perfect order?

10. What are the responses that can be given to overshipping?

11. What are some issues that can occur with on-time delivery?

11

Customer Satisfaction

Why is it important to be concerned about customer satisfaction? The answer is that this is the method that can be used to tell if your customers will continue to purchase your products or services.

ISO 9001:2000, Section 8.2.1 Customer satisfaction, says the following:

> As one of the measurements of the performance of the quality management system, the organization shall monitor information relating to customer perception as to whether the organization has met customer requirements. The methods for obtaining and using this information shall be determined.

ISO/TS 16949:2002, Section 8.2.1 Customer satisfaction is the same as ISO 9001:2000. Section 8.2.1.1 Customer satisfaction—Supplemental adds:

> Customer satisfaction with the organization shall be monitored through continual evaluation of performance of the realization processes. Performance indicators shall be based on objective data and include, but not be limited to:
>
> - Delivered part quality performance
>
> - Customer disruptions including field returns
>
> - Delivery schedule performance (including incidents of premium freight)
>
> - Customer notifications related to quality or delivery issues
>
> - The organization shall monitor the performance of manufacturing processes to demonstrate compliance with customer requirements for product quality and efficiency of the process.

With companies being requested to be registered to either the ISO 9001:2000 standard or ISO/TS 16949:2002 for automotive businesses, customer satisfaction measurement has become an important issue. In years past this was an issue that was not really very important and was very infrequently measured. In today's global market the measurement of customer satisfaction is very important in order to really understand customer requirements and the business itself.

SURVEYS

One of the more popular ways of measuring customer satisfaction is by using a survey. Satisfaction surveys are a tool to collect data about what a customer thinks and feels about your products or services. The development of the survey is critical since you need to be sure that you are collecting the information that you really want. The questions need to be worded so that the customer understands them and responds to them the way that you intend. Care must be taken to understand the entire process and any bias that may be present. This can help clarify data interpretation.

A survey should always be short and specific. This way the customer will be more likely to answer and return the survey. One of the major problems with any survey process is the low rate of return of the surveys. In some cases a good return is only 2.5 percent of those sent out. If you have only a few customers the number returned will be very low, and then the question becomes how to get reasonable data.

A survey can have many different types of questions. Questions can be open-ended, or a Likert scale can be used to rate a series of statements. If a Likert scale is used for evaluation it should always consist of an odd number of possibilities. An example of a Likert scale consisting of an odd number of choices is:

1	2	3	4	5
Strongly disagree	Disagree	Neutral	Agree	Strongly agree

Another example might be:

1	2	3	4	5
Poor	Fair	Acceptable	Satisfactory	Exceptional

By using a Likert scale mathematical values can easily be applied to the results and many different statistical analyses can be performed. Some of these might be percent in each category, mean, standard deviation, and so on.

One fact that you need to remember is that if a response falls in the lower portion of the Likert scale it is going to be very hard to move that customer past the middle. For some reason the customer's expectations have not been met. A detailed investigation of this customer will need to be done to try to understand and identify the expectation that was missed and then develop a process that will meet or preferably exceed this expectation. This can be a long and tedious process because many of the customers that fall in this range may feel that no matter what changes are made, they will never be satisfied. Then the question becomes how much time and money is the supplier willing to spend to work with this customer.

On the other end of the scale you have those customers whose needs are being met and are satisfied with your business. It is important to determine what percent of the responses are on this side of the scale. This ratio gives you a good idea if you have more satisfied than dissatisfied customers. You hope that they will all be satisfied, but mistakes get made that can impact the operations of the customers. One area that needs to be considered is how the supplier responds in these types of situations. The survey results can be used to drive a continuous improvement process to work more effectively with the customer and better meet their requirements.

The biggest and easiest way to improve business performance is to focus on the respondents that chose 4 out of 5. What will it take to make these customers rate you at a 5? This is easier to find out because you already have a satisfied customer that should be willing to work with you so you can get a better understanding of how your business could improve and really benefit the customer. These are typically your larger, faithful customers so you really should be working to get even more business from them. In most cases this is a much easier job than trying to get a new customer or even working with a dissatisfied one. Working with your satisfied customers is a solid way to improve your business performance with the least amount of effort.

Remember the statistic that a satisfied customer might talk to three or four people where a dissatisfied customer will talk to at least sixteen people? Dissatisfied customers want the world to know of their displeasure.

Let me use a personal example. When our children were small we purchased a new car (a Chrysler product). It was a four-door vehicle. When we were driving down the road the back door came open. This was before seat belts and childproof doors. I took the car back to the dealership and I was told that there was nothing wrong and nothing could be done. I wrote a letter to Chrysler Corporation and they sent a representative out to observe the defect, and I was told again that there was not a problem and there was nothing that Chrysler could do. They tried adjusting the door but it did not solve the problem. I left very frustrated and felt very unsafe with this vehicle and also believed that Chrysler Corporation was very irresponsible. I took the time to write one more letter, to the president of Chrysler, and my response was a post card saying that he was sorry I was having problems with my vehicle. I traded the car in for another manufacturer's and have not even considered another Chrysler product in more than 30 years because of the behavior of the company. My final response was to write a thank-you note to the president for this experience, which I would share with others for many years to come. I have used this example since in many presentations around the world. I am sure this has cost them many dollars in business because of their treatment of one customer.

A side note to this example is that there was a town hall meeting in February 2007 arranged by Charles Gibson to discuss the state of the automobile industry today. One of the statements that was made was "it has taken almost an entire generation for the American people to lose confidence in your products, it will take that and maybe more to gain the confidence of the American people back. Can these three (Ford, General Motors, and Chrysler) survive?" That is a tough question and it needs to be dealt with very seriously. The transplant companies care about customers and deliver an excellent product.

Some customers think that they can rule their suppliers. Demands for price reductions, cost savings, a given defect rate or penalties are incurred, and so on, are examples of these behaviors. This is what some of the domestic automobile manufacturers are doing. They have implemented a program of containment and sorting if any bad products are received, which adds to the costs of the supplier significantly. The categories of this program are:

- CS1—After the product is completed, a 100 percent inspection by the supplier is completed before releasing the product for shipment.

- CS2—This level is CS1 plus the material is shipped to an outside company that completes another 100 percent inspection. These charges are all incurred by the supplier.

- CS2 Enhanced—This level is CS2 plus a quality engineer from the customer is there to help resolve problems. Again, more costs for the supplier.

As the costs continue to rise, where is the point where you drop the business? This is what is happening in many cases today.

The concept that the transplant companies are using is working with their suppliers to help them to be able to effectively meet their requirements. If a mistake is made the customer sends engineers to help the supplier identify the root cause, fix it, and be able to deliver top quality products. The customer bears these costs because they value the supplier.

QUESTION DEVELOPMENT AND SURVEY IMPLEMENTATION

Another issue to be considered when using a survey is the questions that are being asked. Before you develop any questions you must have some idea of what you want to measure or what types of responses you expect. Once you define the responses that are expected, then you can begin to develop questions that should give you the responses you are expecting in each area. Before implementing a survey, it should be tested on a sample of people to see if the questions are interpreted the way that you expected. Once the tests validate your survey then it can be used to collect data.

In order for a survey to give meaningful data the sample of respondents must be chosen randomly. This may be difficult to do depending on how the survey is implemented.

Let's look at a comment card for a hotel as an example of a customer satisfaction survey. What kinds of questions are asked? One card had the following types of questions on a 3–5–7 point scale:

- Room

  - Price/value

  - Appearance/cleanliness

  - Everything in working order

- Other facilities

  - Pool

  - Lobby

  - Parking lot

  - Exercise room

  - Business services

- – Internet connections
- • Front desk
  - – Appearance
  - – Friendliness of personnel
  - – Efficiency of personnel
  - – Helpfulness of personnel
  - – Service
  - – Responsiveness to requests
  - – Messages
  - – Wake-up calls
- • Housekeeping
- • Maintenance
- • Management of property
- • Bathrooms
  - – Cleanliness
  - – Amenities provided
- • Continental breakfast
  - – Quality presentation
  - – Cleanliness
  - – Friendliness of personnel
- • Restaurant
  - – Quality of food/beverage
  - – Cleanliness
  - – Quality of service
  - – Quality of room service

All of this is useful information to have about the facility. Who fills out comment cards? Most of the time it is a client that has had a bad experience and the card is being used to register their complaint. This does not provide a random sample of data to analyze to try to effectively evaluate performance in the eyes of the customer.

One solution that I have seen to the random sample problem is to have five to 10 questions that all guests are asked as they are going through the checkout process. This produces a 100 percent sample and a more accurate indication of what the guests think can be evaluated.

The other issue I have with hotels in particular is they are not always asking the right questions. Information about the hotel is nice but when I stay in a hotel I expect a comfortable bed and I expect to get a good night's sleep. Most hotels do not ask these questions yet they are customer expectations that need to be met.

So far we have looked at a service industry; now let's look at a manufacturing questionnaire. Figure 11.1 is a very simple survey that has been used to collect customer satisfaction data.

Notice that there are three critical segments to this survey. The survey can be modified to include other areas that may be important to your business.

One reminder is that people do not like to fill out surveys without some type of reward. If you want a response the survey must be short and very easy to complete and return. Even then the response rate will still be very low. I have seen good response rates of three to five percent of surveys returned.

A graduate student sent me a request for information dealing with quality systems and standards. It was 100 questions and would take 45 to 60 minutes to complete online. This was a survey that I did not complete because I could not sit and wait at the computer for that long during his data collection time. This is a survey that will get a very small number of responses due to the length and time involved.

Open-ended questions can be a good method of getting to the real feelings of the customer. These are much harder to evaluate, however, as all of the responses must be collected and then an affinity diagram developed so the common themes of the comments can be understood.

Why measure customer satisfaction? Collecting this type of information, and understanding customers' needs and desires, can help drive continuous improvement.

There are many other ways that organizations can measure the satisfaction of their customers other than a survey. Some examples are:

- A design firm that has only a few multiyear contracts can use the action lists from status meetings as an indication of customer satisfaction.

- A prototype shop might use the customer sign-off sheets as a measure.

- Customers lost in a given time frame could be used as a measure.

Customer Satisfaction Survey

Customer: _____   Date sent: _____

Plant: _____

You are requested to fill out the following survey. Your response will be used to assess customer satisfaction in the areas of cost, quality, and delivery. Please circle the number that represents your assessment of this company's performance.

Please respond within two weeks from the above date. If your response is not received within this time, the average rating will default to four (4).

Strongly agree	Agree	Neutral	Disagree	Strongly disagree	
					Quality and Cost
5	4	3	2	1	Supplier provides products/services with minimal rejections or quality concerns (overall quality meets needs and requirements)
5	4	3	2	1	Supplier has competent staff to provide the products/services required
5	4	3	2	1	Supplier offers recommendations for continuous improvement and total cost reduction
5	4	3	2	1	Supplier works effectively with plant personnel to manage industrial materials inventories within customer's commodity responsibility (if applicable)
					Delivery
5	4	3	2	1	Supplier shipment performance meets agreed-to delivery timing
5	4	3	2	1	Supplier provides products/services in quantities ordered (without over/under shipments or discrepancies)
5	4	3	2	1	Supplier responds promptly to urgent (emergency) plant supply needs
5	4	3	2	1	Products and services are labeled to meet your/government guidelines and conform to your health and safety requirements.

See over.

Note: For scores of three (3) or lower, detail your concerns so we may develop a corrective action plan.

Figure 11.1   Example customer satisfaction survey.

- Some customers create reports on supplier performance and send these to their suppliers. These can give a very good indication of the issues that may be present with that specific customer.

- Repeat customers give an indication of satisfaction.

- Number of customer complaints can be used. If this indicator is used it is being assumed that everyone that is dissatisfied will complain and if they do not complain, they must be satisfied. These assumptions may or may not be valid depending on the products or services being offered. If the product or service being offered is very expensive, these assumptions will probably be valid. If the product or service is inexpensive (for example, a toothbrush) what may happen is that some will complain, but many will just discard the item they are dissatisfied with and buy a different brand. As a result you may not realize that customers are not satisfied until sales numbers drop, which is actually a lagging indicator.

- Letters or e-mails that are sent to thank an organization for good service and going the extra mile to help a customer indicate satisfaction.

CUSTOMER NEEDS IDENTIFICATION

Let's look at identification of customers' needs. How do you identify customers' needs? Do they all have to get spelled out specifically in a contract? The customers' needs are both spoken and unspoken, and both of these types of needs are requirements that are expected to be met by the customers.

Let's start by looking at the definition of quality. How would you define quality? Each one of us will develop a definition that will work for us and will probably not be the same as someone else's. Let's look at the definitions that the quality gurus and others have developed:

- Dr. Joseph Juran: "Fitness for use."

- Dr. W. Edwards Deming: "Nonfaulty systems."

- Philip Crosby: "Conformance to requirements."

- Tatsuhiko Yoshimura: "Estrangement from expectation of user."

- American Society for Quality: "Quality is a subjective term for which each person has his or her own definition. In technical usage, quality can have two meanings: (1) the characteristics of a product or service that bear on its ability to satisfy stated or implied needs and (2) a product or service free of deficiencies."

- Armand Feigenbaum: "Quality is a customer determination which is based on the customer's actual experience with the product or service, measured against his or her requirements—stated or unstated, conscious or merely sensed, technically operational or entirely subjective—and always representing a moving target in a competitive market."

I prefer to look specifically at Feigenbaum's definition. He brings out more of the aspects of the customer's needs.

In many instances, I use an exercise to help illustrate how much we can take for granted about our requirements as a customer. The exercise requires a group of people to develop the specifications for an object (such as a high chair, camping cooler, bicycle, and so on). Every group that has done this exercise approaches it in a different way because each of us has a different mind picture of the object and what is important.

After the specifications have been developed, the specifications are passed to another group. These are then evaluated to see if there might be areas where more information might be required to be able to produce the product.

I am always amazed at the results. It is an eye-opening experience for people as they realize how much can easily be assumed.

We must be careful as we develop specifications so that the supplier really understands our needs and can supply the product that we are really looking for. This takes diligent work to make happen.

Our goal through all of this is to achieve customer satisfaction. This is a term that can also be hard to define. Let me share a portion of a definition of satisfaction from *Webster's New Universal Unabridged Dictionary* which is: "1. an act of satisfying; fulfillment; gratification. 2. The state of being satisfied; contentment. 3. The cause or means of being satisfied. 4. Confident acceptance of something as satisfactory, dependable, true, etc." As you can see in these four definitions, satisfaction can cover a wide variety of aspects. With such a wide variety of issues that need to be addressed the identification of the customer's needs is critical to the process of satisfying the customer.

A customer satisfaction process may look like Figure 11.2.

Influences impact the customer's prior experience in many different ways. An example of prior experiences would be the expertise of the customer in the product area. Another influencer may be what people are saying about the supplier's organization (word of mouth). Advertising and

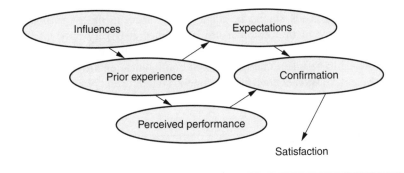

Figure 11.2 Customer satisfaction process.

location of facilities may also have an influence with the customer. As a supplier these influences need to be managed to maintain a positive impression in the marketplace.

From the prior experience, customers develop expectations whether good or bad. The supplier needs to be involved in conversations with the customer so that the unspoken perceptions can be discovered and dealt with.

The next step is the evaluation of the product that the supplier has provided. This is the point where satisfaction gets evaluated. Success at this stage should mean a satisfied customer.

A satisfied customer will not necessarily be a loyal or even a repeat customer. A process needs to be in place to work with the customer to get repeat orders and more business. This is the area where supply chain management principles come into play, like relationship-building and good business management practices. By practicing good management, suppliers can be healthy and around for many years. Developing customer loyalty is crucial in business today since there are many options available from many different companies for the same or similar products.

CONCLUSION

Customer satisfaction measurement is a tool that is required by the quality standards and can be used as a way to drive continuous improvement in the business. It is a mechanism that can help keep organizations competitive in the global market that exists today. There are many ways to measure customer satisfaction, and companies need to develop the best way that will work for them and provide data that indicates the feelings of their customers.

Customer needs should be identified as specifically as possible so that the desires of the customer are being met. It is very easy for both organizations to make assumptions when specifications are being developed. Care needs to be taken that the lines of communication are open and the desires of the customer are truly understood so the correct product is able to be delivered.

KEYWORDS

Customer satisfaction surveys

Likert scale

Question development

Customer comment cards

Customer satisfaction

Customer needs

DISCUSSION QUESTIONS

1. What drivers are there to measuring customer satisfaction?

2. What different methods are there to indicate customer satisfaction?

3. What considerations need to be made when developing a survey?

4. How can the survey response rate be improved?

5. How should survey questions be developed?

6. How should a survey be tested to see if the responders are interpreting the questions correctly?

7. Why would you want to make sure that customer needs have been identified?

8. List some influences that can impact customer satisfaction.

9. Can complaints be used as a measure of customer satisfaction? If they are used, what considerations should be made?

12

How to Apply Basic Quality Tools to Customers and Suppliers

The basic quality tools can be used in many different applications. One of these applications is supply chain management. The tools will be defined and then the application of the tools to supply chain management will be demonstrated. The tools that will be covered are:

- Scatter diagrams
- Histogram
- Tally sheet
- Pareto analysis
- Cause-and-effect diagram
- Control chart
- Five whys
- Brainstorming
- Process map (flowchart)
- 5W2H process
- Affinity diagram

SCATTER DIAGRAMS

Scatter diagrams are used to test a relationship between two different variables. There are many relationships that can exist between variables. Some of these include positive relationship, negative relationship, no relationship, weak positive relationship, and weak negative relationship. There can also be troughs and peak-type relationships between variables.

Scatter diagrams can be used in supply chain management to better understand your own process and its relationship to the finished product. For example, in the coal tar business there is essentially no quality control or specifications on the material. If you buy it you get whatever material comes off the coke ovens. The actual product that is being made is a binding material used in metal smelting processes so there are some very specific requirements that must be met. By analyzing the raw material and the finished product, a scatter diagram can be plotted to see what parameters impact the final product. One of the parameters that is critical to the customer is ash content. By use of a scatter diagram, it was learned that the higher the incoming ash content, the more the tar had to be blended to get the correct ash content in the finished product.

By using scatter diagrams, problem relationships can become apparent. For example, when a specific percentage of boron is in a piece of steel, it will crack. A scatter diagram can help us determine what level of boron can be present and still have the material function successfully. Many times the use of scatter diagrams helps better define customer requirements and specifications.

The process to construct a scatter diagram is:

1. Decide what parameters might be related to each other or that the customer wants to know about.

2. Develop a data collection plan that will collect the required variables.

3. Plot the data with each axis being one of the variables.

4. Observe the plot and see what type of relationship might exist between the variables.

The example that comes to mind again is the amount of ash in coal tar. The question became, is the time in the coke oven (coking cycle) related to the amount of ash that shows up in the coal tar? Data was collected on the ash content in the tar and the coking cycle times. A diagram was created and a positive relationship was shown. This means that when the steel and foundry businesses slow down, the ash content in the coal tar will increase because the coking time will be lengthened. By understanding this concept and relationship, it helped coal tar suppliers to better manage their business with the metal smelters. This is an example of how a change in a supplier's operation can impact the customer. This is an example as well as to why a good communication process between customers and suppliers needs to be developed and maintained.

Scatter diagrams can be used to check for relationships between variables within an organization as well as between organizations. As these relationships are revealed and understood, process improvements can be made and products will be improved. The value of this tool is in the improvements that can happen once relationships are understood.

HISTOGRAM

A histogram is a picture of the distribution of data that are being investigated. It is a bar graph that has the data points grouped together so that a curve of the distribution can be developed. The number of columns that should be used can be found in tables in many statistics books. I have also used the square root of the number of samples rounded to the nearest number to determine the number of bars that should be in the histogram. A normal bell-shaped curve for the distribution is called a normal distribution. There are some statistical rules that apply to normal distributions that can simplify the analysis of these distributions. A picture of the distribution of data can make sorting apparent. If you create a histogram of a critical dimension on a product, you will be able to identify the center point of the data, which is an indication of the center of the supplier's process. Where is this center point in relation to the customer's specifications? As a customer this can be a tool to help understand the performance of the supplier.

I once had a situation where the histogram for the thickness of plates being stamped looked very strange. I went to the manufacturing area and found that the operation had two machines stamping plates and the products from both machines were going into one bin. That was the explanation for the strange looking histogram. This graphical tool gives an indication of how the variability in the process is distributed.

As a histogram is produced, draw in the specification lines on the graph. If you see that the specifications fall at the edges of the histogram and nothing is beyond the specifications it is an indication that sorting is going on by the supplier. I realize that this means that as a customer you may not be receiving out-of-specification material but it is an indication that out-of-specification material is being produced and this is adding costs to the process at the supplier. This is an area that can be improved to remove some costs from the supply chain.

The procedure for the development of histograms is described in detail in statistics books as well as books that specifically deal with the basic quality tools.

TALLY SHEET

This quality tool is used as a method for data collection. A tally sheet can be process-specific to collect the specific data that are needed. I have also seen these with pictures where the defects are marked on the pictures. In the case of a washing machine, each defect was marked on a picture of the machine. As a result it was learned that damage was primarily occurring at one corner. The packaging of the product was redesigned so that the corner where the damage was occurring was strengthened and the problem was eliminated. The picture helped locate the specific area of the problem. Other types of tally sheets may consist of a set of tick marks that almost look like a histogram. With this type of information a broad view of the distribution pattern can be seen. Tally sheets come in all different forms and can be designed for specific purposes. A tally sheet is a way of starting to organize data.

Below is a table of data where the thickness of a part is being measured.

0.247	0.254	0.268	0.261	0.231
0.241	0.252	0.258	0.266	0.226
0.263	0.242	0.242	0.264	0.218
0.216	0.266	0.266	0.218	0.269
0.260	0.241	0.250	0.246	0.245
0.260	0.278	0.260	0.224	0.224
0.222	0.242	0.244	0.277	0.222
0.260	0.249	0.250	0.251	0.255
0.247	0.250	0.235	0.258	0.251
0.245	0.239	0.248	0.271	0.276
0.268	0.230	0.243	0.225	0.232
0.254	0.242	0.248	0.236	0.262
0.223	0.240	0.222	0.261	0.244
0.249	0.226	0.232	0.250	0.248
0.252	0.251			

Now let's convert this data to a check sheet–type format and see what we can learn.

0.216	/	0.237		0.258	//
0.217		0.238		0.259	
0.218	//	0.239	/	0.260	////
0.219		0.240	/	0.261	//
0.220		0.241	//	0.262	/
0.221		0.242	////	0.263	/
0.222	///	0.243	/	0.264	/
0.223	/	0.244	//	0.265	
0.224	//	0.245	//	0.266	///
0.225	/	0.246	/	0.267	
0.226	//	0.247	//	0.268	//
0.227		0.248	///	0.269	/
0.228		0.249	//	0.270	
0.229		0.250	////	0.271	/
0.230	/	0.251	///	0.272	
0.231	/	.0252	//	0.273	
0.232	//	0.253		0.274	
0.233		0.254	//	0.275	
0.234		0.255	/	0.276	/
0.235	/	0.256		0.277	/
0.236	/	0.257		0.278	/

The above table gives a picture of the raw data. Now let's combine some of the data and see what we can learn.

0.210–0.219	///
0.220–0.229	/////////
0.230–0.239	////////
0.240–0.249	/////////////////////
0.250–0.259	//////////////
0.260–0.269	///////////////
0.270–0.279	////

The largest group of data fall in the range from 0.240–0.249. This is an indication that the center of the operation is in this area. This looks like mixed output. This is the type of data that will be observed with two machines feeding into the same process. One machine is making thicker material and the other is making thinner material. Without the combining of the ranges, this would not be visible.

As a result of converting the data to a histogram it is much easier to see what the data looks like and see the range that the data covers. It becomes much easier to make decisions with the data in this more usable format.

PARETO ANALYSIS

Pareto analysis is a method for prioritizing problems based on the ones that occur most often. It is a form of a bar graph. The data are recorded for problems and then put in a table from highest to lowest occurrence. Percentages of the total are calculated as well as cumulative percents. The actual numbers or the percents are plotted on a graph and the cumulative percent line is shown above the bars. The problems that happen most often are corrected and then the analysis is completed again. A sample of a form that can be used for this type of analysis is shown in Figure 12.1. A completed example is shown in Figure 12.2.

Normally the first two bars on the graph will cover very close to 80 percent of the issues plotted. This means that the first two problems will eliminate 80 percent of the issues when they get fixed or corrected. The value of a Pareto analysis is that it has the capability to help direct priorities to the most important areas first. Without this tool it is easy to get preconceived ideas of what the major problems are and go ahead and fix those while they may not be the big problems. This tool helps to create a focus on the correct problems to be resolving.

I have seen this type of analysis used in supply chain management in several ways. One is to determine which material should be looked at for consolidation or replacement. The products are selected and then the chart can be drawn up in pounds and/or dollars to determine the priorities. I have used both so that I can see any significant changes in the charts. This is a very useful tool to help with managing costs as well. The costs that make up a product price can be analyzed by Pareto analysis to see which are the major ones and then you can begin to look at reduction possibilities.

Pareto Analysis—Computation Sheet

Rank	Categories	Data	%	% accum. of total
1				
2				
3				
4				
5				
6				
7				
8				
9				
10				
11				
12				
	Total			

Figure 12.1   Blank Pareto analysis sheet.

Pareto Analysis—Computation Sheet

Rank	Categories	Data	%	% accum. of total
1	Surfactants	7500	63.8	63.8
2	Bases	1800	15.3	79.1
3	Polymers	1000	8.5	87.6
4	Fragrances	600	5.1	92.7
5	Dyes	500	4.3	97.0
6	Acids	300	2.5	99.5
7	Solvents	60	0.5	100.0
8				
9				
10				
11				
12				
	Total	11760		

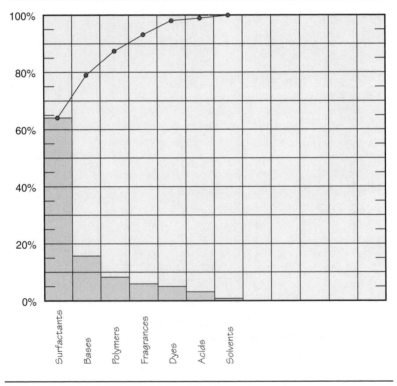

Figure 12.2 Completed Pareto analysis sheet.

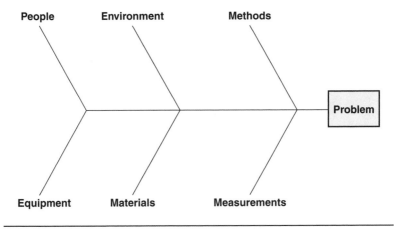

Figure 12.3 Sample cause-and-effect diagram.

CAUSE-AND-EFFECT DIAGRAM

This is also known as the "Ishikawa diagram" or the "fishbone diagram." It is a method for helping to find the root cause of a problem. Various areas need to be considered as the major bones of the fish. These are generally broken into six categories: methods, measurements, people, equipment, materials, and environment. The problem is placed in a box on the right-hand side of the diagram. Then each of the main areas are brainstormed to come up with things that could cause the problem in the box. Each idea is placed as a sub-bone on the diagram. Once the brainstorming session is over, the diagram is analyzed and the possible root cause of the problem is identified. Then the solution is developed and implemented. An example of the starting point of a cause-and-effect diagram is shown in Figure 12.3.

CONTROL CHARTS

There are two types of control charts: variable and attribute.

Variable Control Charts

Variable charts are the most common and are a plot of a measurement over time. Statistical techniques are applied to process data to determine if the variation in the measure is due to common cause variation or special cause variation. A special cause can be identified and corrected, but common cause variation is built into the process and can not be removed unless the process is changed. Control charts give a history of process performance but also help the operators decide when a change or adjustment to the process is necessary.

There are two types of variable control charts. They are the $\bar{X}$ and R chart and the $\bar{X}$ and s chart.

$\bar{X}$ and R Chart

This is the most common variable control chart. The principles that were developed by Shewhart are applied to the data and the statistical calculations for mean and control limits are completed. To be in statistical control a process must fall within ± three standard deviations from the mean of the data. At least 25 data points are necessary to calculate the control limits for a process. Once the control limits have been calculated, they stay the same unless a change has been made to the process. If a data point falls outside the calculated control limits a special cause is sought out for the variation. This control chart uses the constants that were developed by Shewhart to estimate the standard deviation of the data. The formulas that are used and the development of a control chart can be found in any good SPC textbook, therefore I will not be covering that material here.

$\bar{X}$ and s Chart

This form of control chart is very similar to the previous one. The only difference between the two is that this chart is using the actual standard deviation and not the formulas that approximate the standard deviation. With the ease of using statistical software packages today as well as having statistical tools available in Excel, the capability to use this chart is increasing. This chart is completed the same way as an $\bar{X}$ and R chart and the same form can be used. The upper and lower control limits are calculated by adding or subtracting three times the standard deviation from the calculated mean of the data. Plotting of the data is the same for both of these charts.

Attribute Control Charts

Attribute control charts are the second type of control chart. These are prepared from a set of go/no-go type data. One of the issues with attribute charts is that a large data set is required.

There are four different attribute control charts that are used. They are: the p chart, the np chart, the c chart, and the u chart. Let's look at each one.

p Chart

The *p* chart is used to present percent defective. A sample of 100 to 1000 items would be examined for each data point and the percent defective would be calculated and plotted on the chart. This calculation involves taking the number of defectives divided by the number in the sample and then multiplying by 100 to get the percent. The graph can be in fractions or percent. The *p* chart is one of the control charts for attributes that can have a variable sample size due to the ratio calculation from the data. The thing to remember is that when making a *p* chart the sample size should not vary much more than 25 percent from the largest sample size to the smallest sample size.

np Chart

The *np* chart is the raw data that was obtained for the *p* chart. This is a graph of the number of defectives that were observed. As a result the sample size for an *np* chart must be the same for each data point. The format used for this type of control chart is the same as for the *p* chart.

c Chart

The *c* chart is a measure of the number of defects observed. An example of this is the number of defects observed in a square foot of fabric. This chart plots the number of defects identified. As a result the sample size for this type of chart needs to be constant.

u Chart

The *u* chart is a ratio of the number of defects found per another variable like square foot, and so on. This is plotted on the same form as the *c* chart. Since this chart is based on a ratio the sample size can vary for this chart.

Use of Information Provided on Charts

A variable control chart can provide a lot of statistical information. First, if all of the data points lie within the control limits, the process may be in statistical control. There are some other rules that have to be followed that could indicate an out-of-control situation. These rules are covered in SPC texts where chart interpretation is discussed. Once you have a stable process, several types of analyses can be done. The one that I have found to be most useful is to use a *z*-statistic and analyze the data. This way the amount of out-of-specification material that is produced can be calculated. Once a number like this has been calculated, discussions can begin on how it is handled or used so that a reduction process can begin to be implemented. I have found that in the majority of situations where I use control chart information to calculate scrap rates, the customer does not even realize that these calculations can be made from the control chart information. What you are doing with these calculations is gaining a better understanding of the supplier's business and beginning to see where some possibilities for improvement might be. The z-statistic is described in most statistics textbooks as well as in some SPC books.

WHY–WHY DIAGRAMS

This is another tool that is used to find out the potential root cause of a problem. This method starts with the problem and asks "why?" The answers are listed and then you move to these answers and ask "why" again. The answers are listed again. This process continues until you have asked why five times. By the time you have asked why five times you should be very near to the root cause of the problem. This is a process that works well in a team environment.

BRAINSTORMING

This is an idea-generating process. The concept behind this is to generate as many ideas as possible from a group of people. This can be completed "popcorn" style where each person shouts out an idea that is then recorded or it can be more structured by going around the group and having each person suggest an idea in turn. The main thing to remember here is that there are to be no value judgments made on any of the suggestions being offered. They are all to be recorded and the evaluation will come later. This is only an idea-generation phase. Sometimes the off-the-wall idea at first may sound stupid, but in the end it may be the best answer. The brainstorming session can be timed so that as much as possible can be obtained without dragging the process on for what may begin to seem like forever.

This tool works very well in supply chain management when members from companies get together and a problem is presented. What can come from this type of exercise is a stronger relationship and new and creative ways of working together. I have seen this applied to product lines as well, where ideas for new products are the topic of the brainstorming session.

PROCESS MAPS (FLOWCHARTS)

This is a diagram of a complete process. This was covered in Chapter 2 and some examples were shown. A flowchart can be made of almost any process. The detail can be changed depending on the amount of information required.

5W2H

This is a simplified root cause analysis technique. The five W's are *who, what, where, when,* and *why,* and the two H's are *how* and *how many.* If these seven questions are answered, the problem will be specifically defined, with suggestions as to what the root cause might be.

The 5W2H technique can be used to help define a customer complaint or a supplier late delivery or almost any situation that is encountered in the supply chain. Having a specific definition of a problem can go a long way toward being able to develop a true solution.

AFFINITY DIAGRAM

This is a tool that allows ideas to be categorized. A list of brainstormed ideas can be set up in categories so that they are able to be analyzed further and investigated as to the best one to use. Categories are developed and then the ideas are put into the category where they seem to fit best. Then a diagram can be made of the final placement of all the ideas.

Affinity diagrams can be used in supply chain management to help determine methods that may be used to help improve a supplier's performance. This is a tool that will put similar ideas together to see where some relationships might lie. As the groups are developed, new ideas may be generated and then analyzed as to how they can be used to help the supplier.

CONCLUSION

As can be seen, basic quality tools can find application in the process of supply chain management. The tools discussed are used frequently in many other processes as well, but that does not make them any less applicable to supply chain management. Each of the tools has a specific purpose to help improve a process.

KEYWORDS

Scatter diagrams

Histogram

Tally sheet

Pareto analysis

Cause-and-effect diagram

Fishbone diagram

Ishikawa diagram

Control charts

Why–why diagram

Brainstorming

Flowcharts

DISCUSSION QUESTIONS

1. Can you identify an area in the supply chain that can use the scatter diagram as an improvement tool?

2. What are some of the things that can be learned from a histogram?

3. What are some of the things that can be included in a tally sheet?

4. What are some special things that can be learned from a control chart?

5. What is the difference between an attribute control chart and a variable control chart?

6. What does a why–why diagram help to find?

7. How does brainstorming help identify a root cause of a problem?

8. Are all quality tools applicable only to the quality field? Why or why not?

13

Materials Management

The two areas that will be discussed as we deal with materials management are inventory and logistics. Many times the perception of materials management is only as procurement of materials. These other two areas have a significant impact on the overall performance of supply chain management.

INVENTORY ISSUES

How is the proper order quantity determined? This is a question that is not an easy one to answer. There are many factors that need to be considered and weighed as this decision is made. Let's look at just a few of these factors.

First, there is the limitation on the storage space available to store material until it is needed for use. Warehouse space costs money and the potential for damage to the material exists while it is in storage.

Second, there is the question of how much is needed for production and when is it needed. The development of a request for material needs to be understood completely. How this request is developed can determine whether issues come up in the future. The big difference lies in the whether the request is based on a demand number or a forecast number. A demand-based number reflects what has actually been ordered and is needed to produce the requirement. If it is based on a forecast there are no orders that need these materials. The order is being predicted and may not have been received yet. The difference is in what will actually be used. If the forecast is off, the material will end up in inventory.

Third, there is the projected sales forecast for the products that use the material. This helps develop a projected possible usage to see how large the quantity needed may be.

Fourth, there are the price break points that are being offered by the supplier for the material. An analysis will need to be completed by the accounting department to determine if the price breaks that are being offered by the supplier are economical for the business. Will the storage costs end up being more than the savings realized by buying in the larger quantity? The results of an analysis like this can be surprising when all of the costs are considered.

Fifth, there are costs involved in storage of the material while it is waiting to be used. Some of these costs involve the cost of space, working capital that is tied up in the inventory, taxes and insurance on the storage facility, workers to maintain the storage facility, workers to move the material to and from the facility, and so on. It can be easy to miss some of these costs and not create a true picture during the analysis.

Sixth, there is the shelf life of the material being purchased. Many products today have expiration dates on them. Almost all of the products in our grocery stores have expiration dates on them. Products that hit the expiration date have to be removed and discarded in some fashion. The discarding of the product can actually cost money in some cases while in others the product may be able to be disposed of at a reduced price but not used in the original manner. Both of these have an impact on the profit of the organization.

Seventh, there is the order lead time that the supplier requires in order to be able to deliver the product. In a continuous operation enough material will be needed to keep the operation running until the next order is placed and the new material arrives. This time may be able to be reduced by working with the supplier.

Each one of these factors has an impact on the quantity of material that should be ordered. The storage space limitation allows only so much space for material to be stored without getting more space. If this is the case, an analysis of the cost of the additional space versus the cost savings available by buying a larger volume of material should be completed, with all factors involved in the storage process included. One of the main drivers in the volume decision is the amount that has been requisitioned by the production department for use in the production of finished products. The estimated sales volumes should also help to predict the amount of storage necessary and the consumption rate of the material. The price break point from the supplier can be a driver if you are close to a break point. For example, I have seen price reductions for pallet quantities or full truckloads. The question that has to be considered is how long it will take to use up the larger amount of material and how much it will cost to store the material versus buying what is needed and not storing any material. This begins to involve how long the working capital can be tied up before a product is made and can be sold to get the money back. Shelf life of materials must be considered along with the validity of the forecasts. Forecasts need to be accurate within the requirements of the business but they must also reflect the costs that can be incurred. If a material costs $1,800.00 per pound, you must have much closer forecasting of use than if the material cost is $0.01 per pound. Losses and damage from having materials in storage can become very expensive as the price of the material rises. A company that used platinum as a catalyst had to keep an inventory of this material because at the time it was very difficult to get. Due to the value of the material, a security system had to be installed to protect the material from pilferage by employees and others. I have seen fenced-off areas in other facilities used for similar purposes, storing maintenance parts, raw materials, or finished goods. Access is controlled by keys to enter these specific areas.

All of these factors must be weighed and considered for each material to get the best result for your company. There are some formulas that will help estimate and direct your decision but the final result has to be based on the economic requirements of your specific business.

What is the optimal inventory level for a specific business? A term that is used to describe this is *economic order quantity.* Depending on how many of the factors described above are involved, the equation for the calculation can become very complex and involved. The size of orders can be reduced by accepting smaller quantities on each delivery on a more frequent basis. This leads to the just-in-time inventory process. The idea behind this is to minimize the accrual of inventory material that is in storage at your facility and receive mostly material that is going directly to manufacturing or assembly for immediate use.

As more and more companies are attempting to be lean and apply the lean production system, it will be more and more important to manage the inventory process within the organization. Inventory ties up working capital that can't be converted to cash again until the inventory is converted to finished product and then sold to a consumer. This is the main reason that inventory management is a critical issue in managing businesses today. It can be a significant driver in the supply chain management process.

As companies try to lean their supply chain, they use just-in-time inventory to manage their inventories so that the material arrives just as it is needed. There are many different factors that have to be considered when setting up a system like this. Some of these factors are:

- Where is the location of the supplier?

- How frequently can deliveries be made?

- Can my business handle frequent deliveries?

- What additional resources will be needed to handle more deliveries?

- Can I forecast my needs every two to four hours so the supplier is able to meet them?

- What flexibility is available in both businesses to meet the production needs?

- What can cause delays in product delivery?

  - Hurricanes?

  - Winter storms?

  - Truck breakdown?

  - Floods?

  - Fire or explosion at supplier's plant?

  - Others?

The correct level of inventory to accommodate all of these possible delays needs to be developed and maintained by the customer. This is where the importance of the relationship comes into play, as a detailed understanding of both businesses needs to occur.

Inventory management is also a form of cash management. Maintaining inventory requires that there is enough cash available to cover the payment to the supplier for the material that is in inventory. The business needs to continue to operate and make a profit if it is going to remain in business. One of the quickest ways to see a company go bankrupt is to see it run out of working capital. This is the money that is used to pay bills and support the operations. If there is no cash, all of the assets in the world will not help pay the bills today. Working capital can be a good measure of the financial health of an organization, but at times it can be missed when doing a supplier analysis.

What some companies try to do is extend their payment terms so they pay over an extended period of time; thus they are using the supplier's money for a while. This might work for a short time but in the long run it will damage the supply chain. As organizations in the supply chain are not paid and they run out of cash, they may be forced to file for bankruptcy or go out of business. This can destroy the supply chain for many other businesses as well. I saw a situation where one member of a supply chain, a vehicle manufacturer, would not pay their bills for materials. A plastic extruder extended their credit to the limit as he continued to operate and finally was ordered by the bank to cease production until some of the credit was paid. This company was a provider of materials used in the interiors of various vehicles. The vehicle plant wanted to collect damages if their plant went down, but when they would not pay their bills the supply of materials stopped. An article in *USA Today* on February 27, 2007, gave another example of what can happen when bills do not get paid. Ford was cut off from receiving diesel engines for its F-series trucks by International Harvester because their bills had not been paid. There are lawsuits that have been filed and it will probably get very messy in the courts, but what will be the impact on both businesses as a result? Will Ford be able to recover the business that was lost as a result of this action? How will the consumer respond to this situation? These are questions that need to be dealt with by both companies because their credibility with the American people is at stake.

The concept of just-in-time is very good as far as managing inventory in theory, but in reality it may be very hard to implement. Approaching one-piece flow is the ultimate goal of just-in-time and the lean process. I have seen companies that believe that since they have pushed all their costs and responsibilities to the supplier that they are running lean. By doing this, the supply chain has not become lean; the suppler is carrying costs that should be borne by the customer. When developing a lean supply chain you need to consider the entire supply chain and how costs can be removed from every organization and still meet all of the needs. It is easy to focus on just your organization and expect everyone to try to accommodate you.

To make just-in-time systems work requires a very accurate projection of the production requirements of the customer. To accomplish this requires a good forecast. There are many forecasting methods that can be used but they need to meet the requirements and flexibility of the supply chain. Some companies today are posting an estimate of their requirements for the following day on the Internet the night before. These requirements are then updated early in the morning and the morning requests are shipped within the next few hours. This system works well if the variation between the evening and morning projections does not change significantly. What can happen is that the number in the evening changes by a factor of almost two by the morning. If the supplier does not have the inventory, the customer will not get the required amount. If the change results in significantly *less* material being required, the material overage will be held in inventory by the supplier.

Material requirements changing and causing materials to become obsolete is another of the risks involved in inventory holding. This can make an entire stock of material worthless overnight. This causes companies to get into take or pay clauses in contracts so that inventory will not be lost by the supplier. I saw a case where a special material was being eliminated by a supplier. The material that was being eliminated was needed for several of the products that were produced and sold by the customer. A supplier was located that would make the required material but the contract included a clause that all of the material that was produced would be purchased. This was the security that the supplier would not be left with material that could not be used. In other cases I have seen the customer end up paying for the raw materials when special products were involved. There are many ways that arrangements can be made to obtain special products but the best interests of both parties need to be considered.

The typical inventory process before just-in-time looked like a saw blade with ups and downs as the material was used and replenished. The goal under that system was to have the inventory replenished before too many back orders had to be made. The order quantity was calculated to adjust the inventory levels so that the customers got the material when they wanted it. This was a balancing process where the hope was that the customers would accept a small back order while the inventory was being restored and to not create a large amount of dissatisfaction in the customer.

There is much more coverage of this topic in production and operations management texts. These books can be very good resources for inventory management as well as basic principles of forecasting.

LOGISTICS MANAGEMENT

Logistics is a part of the supply chain that often gets ignored or not considered in the process. Logistics is the part of the supply chain that involves the transportation of materials to the various stages in the supply chain. This normally involves trucking companies and warehouses. This is a field that is becoming more important today as large companies are trying to manage their shipping costs. The basis for the different types of freight must be considered. For example, trucking companies use weight to calculate freight, while ocean carriers use volume.

One of the big issues in logistics is at what point in the process does the material change hands. Where does the customer assume ownership of the material and thus all the liability for damage and so on. This can be at the supplier's plant or at the customer's plant depending on how the freight contract is written. The price of the freight is determined by the F.O.B. (freight on board) point in the price quote. The freight is either collect or prepaid. Collect freight means that it is the responsibility of the customer to pay the freight. This is the way to indicate that the customer will take possession of the material when it is loaded onto the truck and headed for their organization's plant. Prepaid freight means that the shipper will prepay the freight company. Sometimes this cost will be charged to the customer depending on the contract. The possession issue is one that needs to be spelled out in the contract for logistics services.

When we think about logistics, we think of trucks initially, but there is also ocean freight as well as railroads. Ocean freight and railroads tend to deal with larger volumes of materials. These need to be considered because for larger volumes they may be cheaper cost-wise, but are the deliveries dependable enough is the question.

With many domestic companies now trying to do business in Asia, the necessity of understanding the implications of ocean freight is increasing. Space on freighters has to be purchased well ahead of time. The freight containers get filled in Asia and shipped to the United States. The container and contents are examined by customs personnel and then the container gets loaded onto a frame that can be trucked or sent by rail to the next destination. As this process is examined, we see that the time involved can be very lengthy and delays can happen at any number of points in the process. For example, a long delay could occur in the customs examination process or the transfer process to the truck or rail car. Each of these can delay the arrival of the material at the final destination. One downside of all of this is that inventory has to be maintained to be able to keep operations running through all of these potential delays. There will be bumps in the road in this process and you need to be ready for them when they occur. It can be very difficult to predict when a shipment from Asia will actually arrive at its destination in the United States.

A term that is becoming more and more popular is *third-party logistics* (3PL). Companies are contracting with logistics suppliers to handle the complete process of getting materials to the right location. With this type of arrangement the logistics supplier can connect with all forms of transportation and take advantage of the best costs. A third-party logistics organization deals with all of the various companies and knows what the rates should be and what can be expected for delivery. This gives the customer the best logistics possible as the experience of the logistics organization is being used to the advantage of the supplier and customer. Many organizations used to have transportation departments that were responsible for handling all of their logistical issues and arranging for all shipments. With the third-party logistics companies coming on the scene these departments are being eliminated in favor of using 3PL providers.

As companies desire to get more and more lean, logistics will be one area that companies are outsourcing to logistics suppliers. I have seen cases where a customer will negotiate a contract with a trucking company for all deliveries to a particular facility. With this type of agreement the suppliers are told to use this trucking company to get materials to the facility. In theory this should reduce the costs for the customer, but the performance of the logistics company needs to be monitored to ensure that deliveries are being handled properly. It is easy to end up with late shipments because a trucker did not deliver as promised and have the supplier blamed for the late delivery. Remember, one of the big issues in the entire supply chain management process is relationships. Efforts must be taken to ensure that relationships are maintained and are growing to be beneficial to both organizations.

Logistics includes any transportation that is done to a product to move it to the next step in the supply chain. This can include ocean freighter, barge, rail, truck, as well as air freight. A logistical supply chain can get complex just like a standard product supply chain. Let's look at an example of how things can change quickly. A raw material was being manufactured in a plant that was only about three hours away from the customer. The material could be stored by the supplier and ordered by the customer as space became available in the raw material storage at the customer. This system was very close to being just-in-time. The supplier decided to go out of the business of making the raw material. The only source for the raw material became Japan, and it had to be ordered in freighter quantities. This quickly created a major logistics problem. Issues like storage volume, lead times, cash requirements, and so on, now came into play. The logistics map expanded to include a freighter to the Gulf of Mexico, transfer to an oceangoing barge to New Orleans, transfer to a river barge going up the Mississippi River to a port on the Ohio River, transfer to trucks to deliver to the plant three hours away. With barge demurrage at $175 per hour, transfer had to be completed quickly and with as many trucks as possible to reduce the costs. It took several freighters full to get the operation figured out so that the demurrage of both the barges and the trucks could be minimized. It was a learning experience that was forced on the organization but they responded and made it work. In another illustration in the automobile industry, suppliers may have to fly parts to assembly plants to keep them from shutting down. Helicopters are rented for this purpose, and I was surprised at how much companies can spend on this type of operation. The suppliers spent enough money that they could have purchased the helicopter and paid the pilot but they had a contract instead. Requiring materials to be shipped by air to keep plants running may not be the best solution for the supply chain when the customer is not very good at relationships.

Logistics is becoming a critical part of supply chain management but was almost ignored as a significant part a few years ago. Some of the characteristics that need to be considered when working with a logistics supplier are:

- What modes of transportation does the organization deal with?

- Will they handle all of the transfers required and documentation necessary?

- Will they see the material through customs and handle any duties?

- Can this organization handle both inbound and outbound freight for you?

- Where is this supplier of logistics located? Where are the hubs set up?

- How much lead time is required by the logistics company?

- Do the employees have the required training to handle the materials that you are shipping?

- How are the various shipping modes insured and who is responsible for any damage?

- How is a damage claim filed? How much paperwork is involved?

- What kind of rates and discounts are available?

These questions will give you a pretty good overview of the logistics company and the capabilities of their organization. The next step may be a visit to the organization or at least to one of the hubs to see what goes on there. This can give you a very good idea of how freight is handled and how orders are moved. The attitudes of the employees will become very obvious as you watch the organization for just a few minutes. Is there care shown for the materials being handled? Are orders prepared ahead of the truck arrival? Is there a schedule of arrivals and departures? Many factors can be revealed with a visit that can be missed when only a discussion in an office is being held.

There are textbooks that have been written on the subject of logistics and these should be used for a reference if more information on logistics is needed.

CONCLUSION

Two important parts of materials management are inventory management and logistics. Inventory management can impact the working capital that the company has and thus the financial health of the organization. Logistics is the transportation that is involved throughout the entire supply chain. These two parts must be considered when a process of supply chain management is being initiated.

KEYWORDS

Inventory

Economic order quantity

Order size

Just-in-time

Warehouse space

Logistics

Ocean freight

Rail freight

Trucking

Air freight

Barge freight

Third-party logistics

DISCUSSION QUESTIONS

1. How does inventory impact the profits of an organization?

2. On a visit to a supplier, would you want to visit the warehouse as well as the production area? Why?

3. How can an order quantity be determined? What are some methods that can be used?

4. What is 3PL and how can it be used?

5. What are some of the benefits of using a third-party logistics provider?

6. Why are logistics important in supply chain management?

7. Why would a company want to have a just-in-time inventory system?

8. What are some things that can happen to materials that are in inventory? What actions can be taken to prevent some of these things?

9. What actions can an organization take to compensate for potential delays that could be incurred at a customs inspection?

10. Why would a company want to import materials?

14

Information Technology Applications

Information technology is moving at a very rapid pace today. New applications continue to be developed and implemented in many different fields, including supply chain management. Information technology is changing the way that business is conducted. In some industries, as the integration of multiple forms of information technology are implemented, much of the old paper systems are replaced with electronic transactions. As information technology advances we must still remember the personal relationships that may be required to make supply chain management work effectively. It could be very easy to let software programs attempt to manage the supply chain but this will not work. Software packages may make some of the aspects of the supply chain management process easier but human relationships play an important part in the management of the supply chain.

A flexible supply chain is important today because it needs to be adaptable to the changes that are happening all around. As new software applications are developed the supply chain needs to be able to accept them and be able to reap the benefits that they create for the businesses. Sometimes the new software may be able to create a competitive advantage for a business. If the software package fits into the business strategy that has been developed for the supply chain then the software may create a competitive advantage for the supply chain. The idea that just because the competition is using a software package it would be better for my business to use the package too will not prove to be a wise decision in the long run. If the software is investigated and it is determined that it will help improve the supply chain management process and improve the performance of your business then it may be a wise decision to try the software package. The entire process of software selection needs to be rigorous so that the best functional software can be obtained. The supplier selection process as well as the needs determination that has been described earlier should be completed before a decision to use any software package is made.

Computers and the technology they offer can improve the efficiency of business operations, and to remain competitive today it is necessary to be able to accept new technology and be able to adjust the business to benefit from this change. Remember that every time an improvement or change is made to the information system within an organization, it should have been observed in another operation. Do not just take a salesperson's word for how much it will save the company or how the benefits will help the organization. An evaluation must be run by the organization to determine if the software would effectively fit into the organization. The process of evaluating software packages can take a significant amount of time. For several of the projects that I have been involved in using software packages, we had to pick several potential packages and then visit the software houses to verify the support base that was available for the package. This was a critical point because management wanted to make sure that if money was spent, the package will not be obsolete tomorrow or in the near future. Management wanted a quick turnaround if problems occurred and by visiting the software house we were able to see what type of support was available. While we were at the software houses we were able to observe how they used and improved the software applications and how many support staff were available.

The attitude that "my business is different and no software package will work for me" is setting you up for a major investment and a very long project that can involve a tremendous amount of scope creep as more and more things come up. Each new form may need to be custom-designed, which can be costly. A good software need definition should be completed before any coding can begin. Commitment by top management to complete the project must be there. I have seen many projects related to information technology abandoned because they overran on both money and time and did not produce what the project set out to accomplish. Care needs to be taken in this area.

For many years a purchase order had to be typed on a typewriter and mailed to the supplier. With the help of the Internet an order can be placed almost instantaneously with a supplier anywhere in the world with Internet access. Country boundaries are being dissolved in the business world by the Internet. Software is being developed that resides entirely on the Internet. This brings companies all over the world closer together. Entire supply chains can now be linked together using the World Wide Web. It is much easier to provide accurate demand information to the link in the supply chain that needs it.

A few years ago fax machines were the new way to transfer information quickly via the phone lines. Then the concept of EDI (electronic data interchange), where order information could be transferred to the supplier's computer and processed without the typical paper process, was developed and implemented in many organizations. Many companies are still using EDI to receive orders today. We have moved a long way beyond EDI in just a few years. Today we can handle orders electronically but also, using bar codes and RFID scanners, the receiving departments can automatically match the order with the receipt of the material and make a payment by an electronic bank transfer. This process is so much more efficient and less costly.

Older employees may not want to trust computers or even desire to use them, but this is the wave of the future and the competition will be using the technology, so to remain competitive and in business, changes will have to continue. People are not comfortable with change, but in the rapidly changing field of information technology they are going to have to learn to change or fall out of business. The downside that we must be careful about is that computers are very impersonal. Successful relationships can not be built in an impersonal environment. A balance needs to be developed between the use of available technology and the personal relationships that are required in the supply chain.

One company that relies a great deal on their information systems is Wal-Mart. In order to keep their shelves stocked they have invested heavily in information technology so that they know how many of each product are selling at each location. With the strength of its computer system Wal-Mart is able to work with suppliers to get reduced prices and meet market needs. Wal-Mart understands that empty shelves do not sell products, so they have a very extensive logistics system to keep the store shelves stocked with material.

Up-to-date information technology is a very important aspect of supply chain management today. We will look at several different types of software packages that are available.

MRP APPLICATIONS

The first one that will be described is MRP (materials requirements planning). Here is a definition of materials requirements planning from *Operations Management*, by William Stevenson: "A computer-based information system that translates master schedule requirements for end items into time-phased requirements for subassemblies, components, and raw materials."

This is one of the early software packages developed and it was designed to help integrate purchasing departments and manufacturing areas. This package also helps with the forecasting of needs for finished products.

An MRP system has three sources of input. They are:

1. The master schedule, which specifies what items need to be produced when and in what quantity.

2. The bill of materials, which contains all of the needed parts and pieces to make one unit of finished product.

3. Inventory records, which contain information on the status of each item for a given time period.

These three inputs work together to balance needs and get the products prepared on time so that the customer is satisfied.

Some of the reports that are readily available from an MRP system are:

- *Planned orders.* This includes future orders with their timing and amounts.

- *Order releases.* This is the execution of the planned orders.

- *Changes.* This can include changes to dates or quantities.

MRP systems help companies reduce the level of in-process inventories as well as keep track of material requirements. By using a master schedule, the capacity available can be evaluated and production time can be efficiently allocated to the correct products.

The next generation of software developed was MRPII (manufacturing resource planning). This integrated more of the businesses processes together to make a more efficient process. Some of the areas added were marketing, finance, and manufacturing. One of the new benefits created was the ability to do capacity planning. Manufacturing resource planning has unlimited application potential in almost every type of business. Some of the business environments where MRPII can be successfully implemented are listed in *MRPII—Making It Happen* by Thomas Wallace. They are:

- Conventional manufacturing (fabrication and assembly)

- Fabrication only (no assembly)

- Assembly only (no fabrication)

- Repetitive manufacturing

- Process manufacturing

- High-speed manufacturing

- Low-speed manufacturing

- Make-to-stock

- Make-to-order

- Engineer-to-order

- Complex products

- Job shop

- Flow shop

- Manufacturers with distribution networks

All of these different businesses have the potential to implement MRPII.

ERP APPLICATIONS

ERP (enterprise resource planning) is the next step in the evolution process. It is the integration of financial, manufacturing, and human resources in a single computer system. ERP systems are composed of a collection of integrated modules. Each different part of the business may have its own module. For example, purchasing would have a module and so would accounting.

The thing to remember with ERP is that it is like any other complex software package implementation: it will take significant amounts of resources and time to implement the software, and these requirements need to be understood by top management at the beginning of the implementation. Some of the challenges that have to be faced with the implementation of any software package are:

- It will require many resources and it is a lot of work.

- It is a project that will have to be done within your organization by your people.

- It will end up not being the number one priority of the company.

- It will involve every area of the company. It cannot be handed to one department to implement.

- It requires people to change and do their jobs differently.

All of these issues can lead to the failure of the project if they are not handled properly. This is a project that needs to be managed using good project management skills and have the complete support of top management. An implementation strategy needs to be developed as well as plans for how it will be executed. The implementation strategy may involve bringing the system up a module at a time or it may be to do the entire system all at once. This depends on what the company is willing to take on and support. The implementation plan may play a very big part in the success of the implementation. Management must agree on the implementation plan and then support the plan until the software is implemented.

In a large system like ERP, care needs to be taken as to how the present system data will be integrated into the new system and what and how much of the old system will be needed. The parallel operation time of the new and old systems will have to be defined as well as the determining points of when the new system is acceptable and working properly. Customizing software packages can be expensive and limits your capability to upgrade at a later date if these customizations are not handled correctly. I saw a situation where a company paid to have a software package customized for their application and when the new upgrade for the base software came out the customization had to be completed again. Sometimes the customization can be done external to the base software so that this type of incident does not happen. Mistakes like this can be very expensive and actually are money wasted.

CRM APPLICATIONS

Customer relationship management (CRM) is the current focus of software being developed. Orders can be tracked, and forecasts and projected needs can be estimated. The concept behind this software is to help manage the business so that the customer's needs are always met in a timely manner and the business remains with you as a supplier.

Especially remember that software cannot replace people relationships and these must be maintained even if software is being used to manage the business.

CPFR APPLICATIONS

Collaborative planning, forecasting, and replenishment (CPFR) is based on information sharing between supply chain members in these areas to help make the supply chain more efficient. These areas are the ones that can cause large swings in demand throughout the supply chain if they are not worked on together. By working in a collaborative manner the entire supply chain is able to reduce inventories and reduce money tied up in the supply chain. To make this process work there has to be open sharing by each company. Business plans need to be shared so that the supply chain can work together to the benefit of all of the organizations. The ideal situation would be to have synchronous flow of materials through the supply chain. The idea of synchronous flow is developed and explained in *The Goal* by Eliyahu Goldratt.

CONCLUSION

Information technology can be used to help improve the processes involved in supply chain management. There are many different types of software packages available and the best one for a specific application needs to be evaluated for each company. There is no one-size-fits-all approach that will work well. When purchasing and implementing a software package, the support of top management is a must. The resources for successful implementation must be allocated. Software can enhance the efficiency of processes but the personal relationships need to be maintained.

KEYWORDS

MRP (materials requirements planning)

MRPII (manufacturing resource planning)

ERP (enterprise resource planning)

CRM (customer relationship management)

CPFR (collaborative planning, forecasting, and replenishment)

Implementation

Software packages

Forecasting software

Statistical packages

DISCUSSION QUESTIONS

1. How can information technology benefit supply chain management?

2. What are the three inputs to an MRP system?

3. Will installing more modules in an ERP system create better data? Why? Why not?

4. How has the Internet helped the process of supply chain management?

5. Will installation of a software package that improves your operations efficiency always help with customer and supplier relationships? Why? Why not?

6. What types of businesses can use software packages for improvement?

7. Which of the software packages discussed may be the hardest to implement? Why?

8. What can a statistical package do for data analysis?

9. How can forecasting software help an organization? What should be considered when justifying the purchase of the software package?

15

Supplier Relationships at the Consumer Level

In today's terms, "supplier relationships" may be better known as customer service. Six situations will be discussed and analyzed so a better understanding of supplier relationships and their impact can be developed.

Successful businesses today realize the importance of supplier relationships and customer satisfaction. Those businesses that don't manage supplier relationships may wonder where their business has gone.

Have you ever traveled to a city and had a confirmed hotel reservation? Have you ever arrived to find no room? How was it handled? Have you traveled frequently to the same city? Did you stay at the same hotel? What was your experience? Did they get to know you and get things done quicker and better? Do you eat at the same restaurant often? What happens? Do the people at the restaurant seem friendlier? What are some of your experiences with car dealers? Have you ever had an "interesting" experience with an airline? How was the situation resolved?

There are a wide variety of customer–supplier situations and they can be resolved in many different ways. The good ones I'm sure we will run into again, but the bad ones will be around for a limited time. As we look at supplier relationships we must go all the way to the consumer and make sure that he or she is satisfied with our product and/or service if we are really going to be successful in the market today.

If you try to build a supplier relationship, will it always be very beneficial to both parties?

HOTEL

The first situation we'll analyze involves a hotel. For almost six months I worked on a contract on the other side of the state. I was staying in a hotel during the week and driving only on weekends. I viewed this as a possibility to build a supplier relationship and decided to see what would happen. The people that worked at the front desk initially were very friendly and helpful. I was able to make a reservation and when I would return, most of the information I needed to register was already there. But they could not understand the difference between a single, nonsmoking, first-floor room and a double, smoking room on the second floor. As time went on the staff at the front desk changed. I tried to make a reservation and I was told to come back later because the clerk didn't know how to do it. I was told my reservation would be entered and when I returned it hadn't been put in. The rate that I was charged several times came out wrong and had to be corrected. This was another area where the clerks didn't know what to do. My credit card bill was very interesting.

One morning at this hotel I heard water running for a long time so I went out in the hall to see what was going on and found water coming out from under the door of the room across the hall. The desk clerk was told about the situation but he said that he could not leave his station to go investigate what was wrong. Three hours later, and water now all across the hall and going into two other rooms, the manager shows up. She is very upset and finds that someone has left a shower on. Then the cleanup began.

If I gave you the name of this place, would you stay there? Do you think they understand the importance of supplier relationships? How would you change this situation? Will they continue to be in business?

This business is not special, as many businesses think they are. Some businesses think that if the customers leave they will always be able to get more customers. It really does not matter how customers get treated in the eyes of an organization like this. Poor service is a problem that can be fixed and should be handled. In comparison, take a look at the Ritz-Carlton Hotel that in 1999 won the Malcolm Baldrige National Quality Award for the second time. Quality principles can be applied if management wants to. I have observed some of the behavior of the staff at the Ritz-Carlton and found them all to be willing to go way out of their way to try to satisfy a customer or meet a need.

RESTAURANT

The second situation involves a restaurant. Now let's look at a positive experience. During a six-month period I ate my breakfast at the same restaurant every morning. The second week I was there, as soon as I arrived the hostess seated me in nonsmoking and a waitress brought me a cup of coffee and a table setting. Those people were friendly and helpful. By the end of the six months, they were asking if I wanted my regular meal. These were four to six different people that all cared about their customers. My wife was with me for a week and before the week was out they were bringing juice and coffee to both of us with the table settings. This was a great experience and a joy to be a part of.

If I gave you the name of this place, would you want to eat there? Do you think they understood the importance of supplier relationships? Would you change this situation? Will they continue to be in business?

Let's look at the hotel. As my supplier I am looking for:

- Efficient service

- A clean room (nonsmoking, single, first floor)

- Quiet

- Working phone

- Clean and working bathroom

- Anything else?

In the restaurant I am looking for:

- Good and hot food

- Efficient service

- Anything else?

What do the employees want? To serve me to get money to meet their needs. Can their family situations impact their reactions in the morning? Yes they can, but they need to be able to overcome these issues and deal effectively with their customers.

I have seen managers fire waitresses for being slow and not meeting customers' needs. The better a waitress treats the customer, the larger the tip that may be given. There can be a significant monetary incentive to serve the customer well.

TAXI

The third situation involves a taxi. This situation occurred while I was living in Pittsburgh, Pennsylvania, and I was responsible for a number of plants (from six to 33 all over the United States) for seven years. I started out every Monday morning on my way to the airport to catch a flight. Most of the time I was on my way to Chicago O'Hare. I would call and reserve a cab to pick me up and take me to the airport. After several weeks of having difficulty getting a cab driver to come and pick me up, a driver came and as we were going to the airport he asked if I did this often at this time in the morning. I told him that I did this every Monday and in many cases several other days during the week. He gave me a card with his home phone number and told me that he would be there every Monday and not to call in a reservation anymore. It took a few weeks to build up confidence in him but it worked out well for over three years. On Monday morning I would tell him what other mornings I needed him. By using this driver consistently I received better service and a clean cab and a safe back-road ride to the airport.

What I was expecting from the cab:

- On-time pickup every time

- Safe trip

- Clean car

- Anything else?

What the driver was looking for:

- A way to get consistent money to meet his needs

- End the trip in a position to get the next rider.

- Good tip

All of these were met in this situation and as a result both parties were satisfied and pleased to be working together.

AIRLINE

The fourth situation involves an airline. While I was doing all this traveling, I had to spend a large amount of time in a variety of airports waiting for connections. In this particular case I was waiting at the Nashville airport for four hours. The counter person came to me and said that since I had such a long wait, would I like to use the "special service room." I did not know what she was talking about so she showed me this gray door in the airport that opened into a room that looked like an airline club inside. It had nice furniture and an open refrigerator with some cold nonalcoholic drinks, fresh fruit, and munchies. Believe me, it made the wait go a whole lot faster, and she even came to remind me that my flight was in and that I could board at any time. This was more than I expected from the airline. It was great service and it was good enough that it would make me brag about the service that I had been given.

What was I looking for?

- On-time flight

- Safe trip

- Efficient service

- Courteous attendants

- Anything else?

What are the employees looking for? This is a job to make money to meet their needs.

As a result of this I had a much better respect for the airline and its personnel, and did not struggle with some of the difficulties that were beyond their control. It made my tolerance level for difficulties a bit higher because of the great experience that I had with the one employee.

AUTOMOBILE

The fifth situation involves the purchase of an automobile. I purchased a brand new car in 1975. It was just the car that my family had wanted! Unfortunately, the latches on the back doors were faulty and the doors would not close right. With little children this is a very important thing to have working correctly. I took it back to the garage and they told me that there was nothing wrong with the latches. I wrote to the company and they sent a representative, and he asked me what I expected them to do. I told him that I expected the latches to be fixed. He told me to take it back to the garage and they would fix it. They did absolutely nothing! I had the opportunity to share this event and the handling of it at many meetings involving Toastmasters and other speaking groups. I wrote to the company and thanked them for the opportunity to share my experience with their poor quality and service. They sent me no response. Since it was too much of a bother to safely fix a door latch, I sold the car, and 25 years later neither I nor anyone in my family has had any dealings with that car company.

What did I expect?

- Well-built vehicle worth the price

- Dependable vehicle

- Safe vehicle

- Fast and efficient service

What were the employees looking for? Selling cars to make money to meet their needs and not worrying about someone that has bought one.

This company has lost lots of income over the past years as a result of the behavior of a few employees. These attitudes still exist in auto dealers today and they are losing lots of business because of this behavior and they really don't seem to care. One of the results is the loss of market share to foreign competition, which is growing every year. These are the kind of problems that the Big Three have created and now they have a consumer group that does not want to buy their vehicles. It is going to take many years for these organizations to be able to convince consumers that they should try their vehicles again.

ANOTHER HOTEL

The sixth situation involves yet another hotel. As I was traveling to Chicago every week, I stayed in the same hotel and I made friends with the owner. Even when a travel agency could not get reservations, I could call and get a room for my one night. In one case I was given a suite at my normal corporate rate. This hotel appreciated the business and would go out of their way to make sure that they could accommodate my travels. I always had a room, I had a very easy check-in every week, and I had to provide very little information when I arrived.

Whether you have a good experiences or a bad experience is based on the hotel's view of customer–supplier relationships and the value that they can add to their business.

Who are your suppliers?

- Grocery store

- Bank

- Hardware store

- Lawn service

- Postal service

- Dry cleaner

- Hotel

- Taxi

- Airline

- Restaurant
- Car dealer
- Clothing store
- Many more

At work, who are your suppliers?

- Who provides you with the information to do your job?
- Who provides services needed?
- Secretary
- Receptionist
- Information systems
- Other departments
- Plants
- Others

As you can see, there are a variety of customer–supplier situations that can occur in our lives. As consumers we are looking for the good ones and want to repeat them. The bad situations we do not want to repeat and we would probably not return to the offending business if at all possible.

It can take a long time to win a dissatisfied customer back, if ever. The concept of this was shown when Charles Gibson came to Detroit to do a town hall meeting on the Detroit auto industry. One of the questions that was asked was, "Since the domestic auto companies have worked very hard for the last generation convincing consumers that they do not make quality vehicles, and it will take another generation or longer to convince the consumer to come back, can your company survive?" This is a hard question but it shows that dissatisfied customers have no desire to return and give a company a second chance.

Consumers are the determining factors in the success of any business. If they do not return and you have no customers you will not be able to stay in business.

CONCLUSION

The thing to remember is that the customer is paramount in any business, and they need to be satisfied and loyal to your product. If they are not satisfied, another supplier will be found. What are you and your employees doing to satisfy your customers? This point needs to be remembered—that even though your business does not serve the consumer, the consumer must be made happy or your business will suffer. Relationships in the supply chain are important and can help one better understand the end customer's expectations.

KEYWORDS

Hotel

Restaurant

Taxi

Customer satisfaction

Consumer

Airline

DISCUSSION QUESTIONS

1. Describe a good experience that you have had as a consumer.

2. Describe a bad experience that you have had as a consumer.

3. What would it take to make a bad experience a good experience?

4. Why do you believe that the consumer has to be satisfied?

5. What can you learn from a customer? Can they help your processes improve?

6. What are your expectations at a hotel? Why?

7. What are your expectations at a restaurant?

Bibliography

ANSI/ISO/ASQ Q9001-2000, American National Standard, Quality management systems—Requirements. Milwaukee: American Society for Quality, 2000.

Automotive Industry Action Group. *Technical Specification, ISO/TS 16949, Second Edition, 2002-03-01, Quality management systems—Particular requirements for the application of ISO 9001:2000 for automotive production and relevant service part organizations.* Switzerland: International Automotive Task Force, 2002.

Chopra, S., and P. Meindl. *Supply Chain Management: Strategy, Planning, and Operation,* First Edition. Upper Saddle River, NJ: Prentice Hall, 2001.

Cox, J. F., III, and J. H. Blackstone, Jr. *APICS Dictionary,* Eighth Edition. Falls Church, VA: American Production and Inventory Control Society, Inc., 1995.

Goldratt, E. M., and J. Cox. *The Goal,* Second Revised Edition. Great Barrington, MA: North River Press, 1992.

International Organization for Standardization. *ANSI/ISO/ASQ Q9001-2000, American National Standard, Quality management systems—Requirements.* Milwaukee: American Society for Quality, 2000.

Porter, M. E. *Competitive Advantage: Creating and Sustaining Superior Performance.* New York: The Free Press, 1985.

———. *Competitive Strategy: Techniques for Analyzing Industries and Competitors.* New York: The Free Press, 1980.

Stevenson, W. J. *Operations Management,* Seventh Edition. New York: McGraw-Hill/Irwin, 2002.

Tyndall, G., C. Gopal, W. Partsch, and J. Kamauff. *Supercharging Supply Chains: New Ways to Increase Value Through Global Operational Excellence.* New York: John Wiley and Sons, 1998.

Wallace, T. F. *MRPII: Making It Happen.* Essex Junction, VT: The Oliver Wight Companies, 1985.

Webster's New Universal Unabidged Dictionary, Fully Revised and Updated Edition. New York: Barnes and Noble, 2003.

Wight, O. W. *Manufacturing Resource Planning: MRPII,* Revised Edition. Essex Junction, VT: Oliver Wight Limited Publications, 1994.

Womack, J. P., and D. T. Jones. *Lean Thinking: Banish Waste and Create Wealth in Your Corporation.* New York: Simon and Schuster, 1996.

Index

A

acquisition costs, 20, 21–23
affinity diagram, 167
age, as cultural difference, 108
aggregate planning, 49–50
airline, supplier relationships in, 190–91
American Society for Quality, 151
Amtrak, 49
appearance, as cultural difference, 103
application costs, 21, 26–27
attribute control charts, 164–65
attributes, supplier
    grouping, in supplier
        identification, 76–77
    ranking/weighting, in supplier
        identification, 75
automobile dealership, supplier
    relations in, 191–92
automobile industry, U.S., 4, 6
automobiles, domestic content, 6
autoregressive moving average model
    (ARIMA), 42

B

backward integration, 45

bar codes, 181
bids, processing, as supply chain cost, 23
Big Three, automobile manufacturers, 4, 21, 29, 140, 146
bottleneck operations, as supply chain cost, 28
Box-Jenkins method, 42
brainstorming, 166
    for product improvement, 94–95
brand awareness, in make or buy decision, 57
Brown's exponential smoothing method, 42
buildings, as supply chain cost, 22
bullwhip effect, 41
buy decision drivers, 56–59
buying habits, as cultural difference, 103–4

C

c chart, 165
capacity
    and demand, 49–50
    in make or buy decision, 53–54
cash management, and inventory, 172
cause-and-effect diagram, 163